Gooseberry Patch

Farmhouse Kitchen

A Country Store In Your Mailbox®

Gooseberry Patch
600 London Road
P.O. Box 190
Delaware, OH 43015

www.gooseberrypatch.com

1·800·854·6673

Copyright 2009, Gooseberry Patch 978-1-933494-82-1
First Printing, June, 2009

Do you have a tried & true recipe...

tip, craft or memory that you'd like to see featured in a **Gooseberry
Patch** cookbook? Visit our website at **www.gooseberrypatch.com**,
register and follow the easy steps to submit your favorite family recipe.
Or send them to us at:

Gooseberry Patch
Attn: Cookbook Dept.
P.O. Box 190
Delaware, OH 43015

Don't forget to include the number of servings your recipe makes,
plus your name, address, phone number and email address.
If we select your recipe, your name will appear right along with
it...and you'll receive a **FREE** copy of the cookbook!

Contents

Raspberry JAM

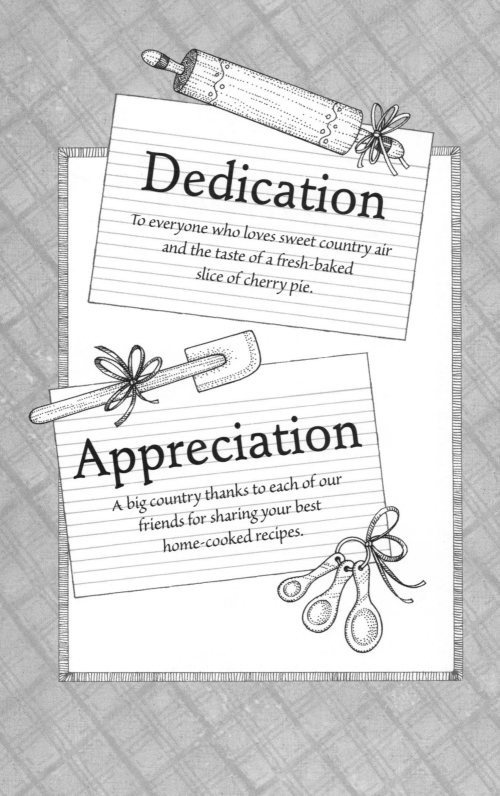

Dedication

To everyone who loves sweet country air
and the taste of a fresh-baked
slice of cherry pie.

Appreciation

A big country thanks to each of our
friends for sharing your best
home-cooked recipes.

Farm-Fresh *Breakfasts*

Grandma Hopkins' French Toast

Farrah Richards
Kinsman, OH

My mom got this recipe from her mother-in-law. I grew up on a farm and we would often have this on Saturday mornings after morning chores. Just knowing that we were going to have French toast afterwards made us do our chores a little faster. Now I fix it for my husband and little boy...they love it too!

2 eggs, beaten
1 c. milk
1 c. all-purpose flour
2 t. sugar
1/2 t. baking powder
1/4 t. salt

1/2 t. nutmeg
1/2 t. cinnamon
8 to 10 slices Texas toast
Optional: bacon drippings
Garnish: maple syrup

Whisk together eggs and milk in a small bowl; set aside. In a large shallow bowl, mix flour, sugar, baking powder, salt and spices. Add egg mixture to flour mixture to make a thin batter. Dip bread slices into batter. Heat drippings, if using, or non-stick vegetable spray on a griddle over medium heat. Fry bread slices on both sides until golden. Serve with maple syrup. Makes 8 to 10 servings.

Start a collection of retro jelly-jar juice glasses...their fun designs and bright colors will make everyone smile at breakfast time.

Farm-Fresh *Breakfasts*

Cinnamon Sticky Buns

Ruby Dorosh
Shippensburg, PA

These yummy buns are a snap to make with frozen bread dough.

1/2 c. brown sugar, packed
1/2 c. molasses
1/2 c. butter, melted and divided

1/2 c. cinnamon-sugar
2 loaves frozen bread dough, thawed

Combine brown sugar, molasses and 1/4 cup butter in an ungreased 13"x9" baking pan. Place in a 325-degree oven until melted. Remove from oven; stir to mix and set aside. Place remaining butter in a small dish; place cinnamon-sugar in another small dish. Pinch off bite-size pieces of dough; dip each piece into melted butter, then roll in cinnamon-sugar. Place dough pieces in pan on top of brown sugar mixture. Cover pan; let stand until dough rises to top of pan, about one hour. Bake at 325 degrees for 35 minutes. Immediately invert pan onto a tray; let sticky glaze drizzle over buns. Makes 8 to 10 servings.

Vintage rotary mixers can be found at flea markets and tag sales. They're oh-so handy for mixing up pancake batter and scrambling eggs quickly and easily.

Betty's Hot Cheese Toast

Connie Chambers
Colorado City, TX

A wonderful friend of mine would always share this scrumptious dish when she hosted our ladies' Bible studies. It is so good...we all loved walking into her kitchen and smelling the hot cheese toast in the oven!

1 c. mayonnaise
2 t. Worcestershire sauce
1/2 t. ranch salad dressing mix
1/4 t. paprika
2 green onions, chopped

2-1/2 oz. pkg. chopped almonds
8-oz. pkg. shredded Cheddar
  cheese
2 T. bacon bits
15 bread slices, halved

Combine all ingredients except bread slices; mix well. Spread on half-slices of bread; arrange slices on a lightly greased baking sheet. Bake for 10 minutes at 400 degrees, until golden. Serve hot. Makes 12 to 15 servings.

A wire basket full of brown eggs makes a terrific farm-style breakfast centerpiece. For a seasonal touch, fill the basket with mini white eggplants or egg-shaped gourds.

Farm-Fresh *Breakfasts*

Hearty Sausage & Egg Bake

Laura Phares
Greenfield, IN

This easy-to-fix dish is always a big hit when I serve it at our church's sunrise breakfast...everyone just loves it!

6-oz. pkg. croutons
2 lbs. ground pork sausage,
   browned and drained
6 eggs, beaten
2-1/2 c. milk

1 t. dry mustard
10-3/4 oz. can cream of
   mushroom soup
8-oz. pkg. shredded Cheddar
   cheese

The night before, sprinkle croutons into a greased 13"x9" baking pan; top with sausage. Beat eggs, milk and mustard together; pour over sausage. Cover and refrigerate overnight. In the morning, spread soup over casserole; sprinkle with cheese. Bake, uncovered, at 300 degrees for one hour, or until center is done. Makes 16 servings.

A buttery slice of cinnamon toast warms you right up on a chilly morning. Spread softened butter generously on one side of toasted white bread and sprinkle with cinnamon-sugar. Broil for one to 2 minutes until hot and bubbly. Serve with mugs of hot cocoa...yummy!

Chocolate Chip Scones

Terry Parke
Indianapolis, IN

*For a tasty variation, use white chocolate chips instead of
milk chocolate...even add some dried cherries or blueberries.*

1 c. sour cream or buttermilk
1 t. baking soda
4 c. all-purpose flour
1 c. sugar
2 t. baking powder
1/4 t. cream of tartar

1 t. salt
1 c. butter
1 c. milk chocolate chips
1 egg, beaten
1 T. vanilla extract
Garnish: sugar

Stir together sour cream or buttermilk and baking soda in a small
bowl; set aside. In a large bowl, combine flour, sugar, baking powder,
cream of tartar and salt. Cut in butter with a pastry blender; mix in
chocolate chips. Add egg and vanilla to sour cream mixture; stir into
dry ingredients just until moistened. Turn dough out onto a lightly
floured surface; roll or pat out into a round about 3/4-inch thick. Cut
into wedges or cut out circles with a large round cookie cutter. Place
on 2 lightly greased baking sheets; sprinkle with sugar. Bake at
350 degrees for 12 to 15 minutes, or until golden. Makes about
one dozen.

*Share your homemade
goodies with a friend. Wrap
scones in a tea towel and
tuck them into a basket
along with a jar of jam.
A sweet gift that says,
"I'm thinking of you!"*

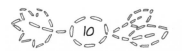

Farm-Fresh *Breakfasts*

Apple-Cinnamon Spread

Francie Stutzman
Dalton, OH

Scrumptious on raisin bread or toasted bagels.

2 8-oz. pkgs. cream cheese,
   softened
1 apple, cored, peeled and diced
1/2 c. raisins

1/4 c. orange marmalade
1/2 t. cinnamon
1/8 t. nutmeg

Combine all ingredients and stir until well blended. Spoon into a
covered container; keep refrigerated. Makes about 3 cups.

I'll tell you how the sun rose,
A ribbon at a time.
-Emily Dickinson

Creamy Ambrosia Salad

Amber Carlson
Irvine, CA

On busy mornings, I love having a big bowl of this sweet, healthy fruit salad ready for my family's breakfast. It only requires a handful of ingredients and takes just minutes to put together.

1/2 c. mayonnaise
1 c. plain or vanilla yogurt
30-oz. can fruit cocktail, drained
20-oz. can pineapple chunks, drained

5-oz. pkg. sweetened flaked coconut
1/2 c. raisins
1/2 c. chopped walnuts

In a large bowl, fold mayonnaise into yogurt. Stir in remaining ingredients. Cover and refrigerate for 2 hours, or until thoroughly chilled. Makes 8 to 10 servings.

Tuck fresh blossoms into vintage soda bottles to line up on a windowsill. Tint the water in the bottles with a few drops of food coloring, just for fun.

Farm-Fresh *Breakfasts*

Peach Cobbler Muffins

Bonnie Allard
Santa Rosa, CA

My most requested muffins...I hope you all like them as much as my family & friends do! Everyone loves them so much, they disappear right away whenever I make them to share.

3 c. all-purpose flour
1 c. sugar
1-1/2 T. baking soda
1/2 t. salt

3/4 c. butter, diced
1-3/4 c. milk
16-oz. can peaches, drained and chopped

Mix flour, sugar, baking soda and salt in a large bowl. Cut in butter with a pastry knife or a fork. Add milk and peaches; stir just until moistened. Spoon batter into greased or paper-lined muffin cups, filling 2/3 full. Spoon topping onto muffins. Bake at 400 degrees for about 20 minutes, or until golden. Turn out and cool slightly on a wire rack; serve warm or cold. Makes 1-1/2 dozen.

Topping:

2 T. butter, diced
2 T. sugar

1/2 t. cinnamon

Mix together in a small bowl until crumbly.

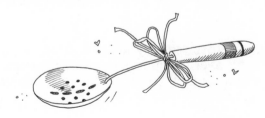

Most muffin batters can be stirred up the night before, and can even be scooped into muffin cups. Simply cover and refrigerate...in the morning, pop them in the oven. Your family will love waking up to the sweet smell of muffins baking!

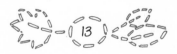

Blueberry-Sausage Breakfast Cake
*Sarah Hoechst
Bismarck, ND*

An all-in-one breakfast that's extra special.

2 c. all-purpose flour	8-oz. container sour cream
1 t. baking powder	2 eggs
1/2 t. baking soda	1 lb. ground pork sausage,
1/2 c. butter	browned and drained
3/4 c. sugar	1 c. blueberries
1/4 c. brown sugar, packed	1/2 c. chopped pecans

In a medium bowl, mix flour, baking powder and baking soda; set aside. In a large bowl, beat butter until fluffy with an electric mixer on medium speed. Add sugars and sour cream; beat until combined. Add eggs, one at a time, beating just until combined. Add butter mixture to flour mixture. Fold in sausage and berries. Pour batter into an ungreased 13"x9" baking pan. Spread evenly in pan; sprinkle pecans on top. Bake at 350 degrees for 35 to 40 minutes, until a toothpick comes out clean. Cool on a wire rack; cut into squares. Serve with warm Blueberry Sauce. Makes 15 servings.

Blueberry Sauce:

1/2 c. sugar	2 c. blueberries
2 T. cornstarch	1/2 c. lemon juice
1/2 c. water	

Combine sugar and cornstarch in a medium saucepan; add water and berries. Cook and stir over medium heat until thickened and bubbly. Cook and stir 2 minutes more. Stir in lemon juice; cool slightly before pouring over cake.

Add a dash of whimsy to the breakfast table...serve up cream or pancake syrup in a vintage cow-shaped creamer.

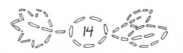

Farm-Fresh *Breakfasts*

Harriet's Potato Pancakes

Harriet Hughes
Wurtsboro, NY

My husband loved to eat one pancake between two buttered pieces of bread with a cup of coffee...anytime! These are so good. I passed this recipe along to our niece who owns a cafe, and they are one of her breakfast hits.

1 c. all-purpose flour
2 t. baking powder
Optional: 1 t. salt
2 eggs, beaten
1 c. milk

2 T. onion, grated
1/4 c. butter, melted
3 c. potatoes, peeled and finely grated
additional butter for frying

In a small bowl, mix together flour, baking powder and salt, if using; set aside. Combine remaining ingredients, except butter for frying, together in a medium bowl. Stir flour mixture into potato mixture until well blended. Drop by tablespoonfuls onto a buttered frying pan or griddle. Cook on both sides until golden. Serves 6.

A hearty breakfast that's welcome on the chilliest morning! Cook up frozen diced potatoes and onions in a cast-iron skillet, then use the back of a spoon to make 6 wells. Break an egg into each and bake at 350 degrees for 12 to 14 minutes, until eggs are set. Add salt & pepper to taste and serve piping hot, right from the skillet.

Crispy Cornbread Waffles

Cathy Clemons
Narrows, VA

I served these yummy waffles when my son and his family came in for the weekend. My grandbabies just loved these with apple butter... I didn't think they would ever get full!

10 slices bacon
1/3 c. oil
2 c. cornmeal
1 c. all-purpose flour
1 t. baking powder
1/2 t. baking soda
1/2 t. salt

2 t. sugar
1-1/2 c. milk
2 T. white vinegar
2 eggs
Garnish: butter, apple butter, maple syrup

Fry bacon in a large skillet over medium heat; remove bacon and crumble. Stir oil into drippings; set aside to cool. In a medium bowl, combine cornmeal, flour, baking powder, baking soda, salt and sugar; set aside. Combine milk and vinegar; let stand for 10 minutes. Beat eggs in a large bowl; add drippings and milk mixture. Add cornmeal mixture and crumbled bacon; mix well. Pour by 1/4 or 1/2 cupfuls onto a preheated waffle iron. Bake until golden, according to manufacturer's directions. Serve with butter and apple butter or maple syrup. Makes about 5 servings.

Waffles with whipped cream and fruit...is there a more delicious way to start a day? We don't think so! Garden-fresh strawberries and blueberries are irresistible...thawed frozen berries are yummy too and available year 'round.

Farm-Fresh *Breakfasts*

Mom's Red Flannel Hash

Phyllis Peters
Three Rivers, MI

This is an old family recipe that has stayed a favorite through the generations. It's a good way to use up leftover cooked potatoes. A real down-home breakfast dish...give it a try!

12-oz. can corned beef, coarsely
  chopped
2 c. beets, peeled, cooked and
  chopped

2 c. potatoes, peeled, cooked
  and chopped
1/2 c. butter, melted

Toss all ingredients together. Pour into a greased 2-quart casserole dish. Bake, uncovered, at 350 degrees for 40 minutes. Makes 4 to 6 servings.

Hard-boiled eggs the easy way! Cover eggs with an inch of water in a saucepan; place over medium-high heat. As soon as the water boils, cover the pan and remove from heat. Let stand for 18 to 20 minutes... cover with ice water, peel and they're done!

Angel Biscuits

Molly Wilson
Rapid City, SD

*My mother would make this up every Sunday afternoon so we could
have fresh-baked bread all week. The dough will keep for
several weeks in the refrigerator.*

2 envs. active dry yeast
1 c. warm water
2 c. buttermilk
3/4 c. oil
1/4 c. sugar

6 c. all-purpose flour
4 t. baking powder
1/4 t. baking soda
1-1/2 t. salt

In a very large bowl, dissolve yeast in very warm water, 110 to
115 degrees; let stand for several minutes. Stir in buttermilk, oil and
sugar. In a large bowl, combine remaining ingredients; stir into
buttermilk mixture. Cover bowl and place in refrigerator overnight.
Remove dough as needed. Roll out on a floured board to 1/2-inch
thickness. Cut out biscuits with a round biscuit cutter or a glass
tumbler; place on an ungreased baking sheet. Bake at 400 degrees
for 12 to 15 minutes, until golden. Makes 4 dozen.

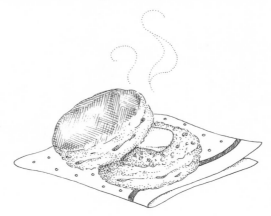

*Shh...here's the secret to flaky homemade biscuits!
Don't overmix or overwork the dough...just stir
to mix and roll or pat out gently.*

Mama's Tomato Gravy

Melissa Dommert
Baytown, TX

My mama, Patsy Marie Paul, made countless batches of biscuits and tomato gravy in her lifetime. I'm sure she learned to make this from her mother, Carmen Inez Shirley. It's a genuine taste of Louisiana Cajun country, where folks are already drinking coffee and eating breakfast by the time the rooster crows.

1/4 c. bacon drippings	5 T. tomato paste
3 T. all-purpose flour	salt and pepper to taste
2 c. water	6 to 8 buttermilk biscuits, split

Heat drippings in a skillet over medium-high heat. Stir in flour and cook, stirring constantly, until lightly golden. Slowly pour water into flour mixture while whisking; whisk in tomato paste. Cook mixture until it begins to thicken. Reduce heat to low and simmer until thick, about 5 minutes. Add salt and pepper to taste. Spoon over biscuits. Makes 6 to 8 servings.

Salt & pepper is a must with scrambled eggs, crispy hashbrowns and other tasty breakfast foods. Look for a pair of rooster-shaped shakers for a sweet rise & shine greeting at the breakfast table.

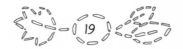

Grandma's Doughnut Holes

Lillian Child
Omaha, NE

My Grandma Karaus brought these fresh, hot doughnut holes to every family gathering. We kids always looked forward to seeing that large brown grocery sack full of these sugary treats!

1-1/2 c. all-purpose flour
1/3 c. sugar
2 t. baking powder
1/2 t. salt
1/2 t. nutmeg
1/2 c. milk

2 T. oil
1 t. vanilla extract
1 egg, beaten
oil for deep frying
Garnish: 1/2 c. sugar,
   1 T. cinnamon

Combine flour, sugar, baking powder, salt and nutmeg in a large bowl; set aside. In a small bowl, whisk together milk, oil, vanilla and egg. Add milk mixture to dry ingredients. Stir with a fork just until dry ingredients are moistened; do not overmix. Heat 3 to 4 inches oil to 375 degrees in a large saucepan. Drop batter by teaspoonfuls into hot oil, 5 to 6 at a time. Fry one to 2 minutes on each side, until deep golden. Drain on paper towels. Mix sugar and cinnamon; place in a brown paper bag. Drop warm doughnut holes into bag; shake until coated. Makes 3 dozen.

Float a blossom inside a 1950's-era egg cup to set
at each breakfast place...so cheerful!

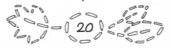

French Breakfast Puffs

Andrea Cullinan
Delaware, OH

My family has always enjoyed these melt-in-your-mouth muffins.
If making mini muffins, reduce the temperature to 325 degrees
and bake for 10 to 12 minutes.

1/3 c. shortening
1 c. sugar, divided
1 egg, beaten
1-1/2 c. all-purpose flour
1-1/2 t. baking powder

1/2 t. salt
1/2 t. nutmeg
1/2 c. milk
1 t. cinnamon
6 T. butter, melted

Blend together shortening, 1/2 cup sugar and egg in a large bowl; set aside. In another large bowl, combine flour, baking powder, salt and nutmeg. Add to shortening mixture alternately with milk; stir until moistened. Fill greased muffin cups 2/3 full. Bake at 350 degrees for 20 to 25 minutes, until golden. Combine cinnamon and remaining sugar. Roll hot muffins in melted butter and then in cinnamon-sugar mixture. Makes one dozen.

Vintage glass measuring cups are a real find at tag sales! Look for them in rosy pink and leafy green tints as well as milk glass and jadeite. Use one-cup measures to serve up cream & sugar...tuck bouquets of freshly cut flowers into oversized 4-cup measures.

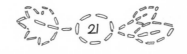

Mom's Everything Waffles

Tamara Ahrens
Sparta, MI

These waffles have been a Saturday morning tradition in our family since our children were very little. If a week goes by without our waffles, we try to slip them in for a weeknight meal. They have developed over time with the addition of many tasty ingredients...even chocolate chips for birthdays and Christmas!

2 c. biscuit baking mix
1-1/2 c. quick-cooking oats, uncooked
1/4 c. wheat germ
1/2 c. chopped pecans or walnuts
2 eggs, beaten
1/4 c. peanut butter
1/2 c. vanilla yogurt
3-1/2 c. low-fat milk, divided
1 c. blueberries
Optional: 1/4 c. mini chocolate chips
Garnish: maple syrup, fruit topping, whipped cream

Combine baking mix, oats, wheat germ and nuts in a large bowl; set aside. In a separate bowl, whisk together eggs, peanut butter, yogurt and 3 cups milk. Add to dry ingredients and stir. Add additional milk if needed to get the consistency of applesauce. Fold in berries and chocolate chips, if using. Pour by 1/2 cupfuls onto a preheated waffle iron that has been sprayed with non-stick vegetable spray. Bake until crisp, according to manufacturer's directions. Serve with maple syrup or fruit topping and a dollop of whipped cream. Serves 4 to 6.

A jar of honey is a sweet addition to the breakfast table to enjoy on hot biscuits, toast or pancakes... even drizzled in a steamy cup of hot tea. For a sweet gift, pick up flavors like orange blossom and wildflower at a farmers' market...be sure to add a wooden honey dipper too!

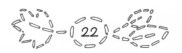

Farm-Fresh *Breakfasts*

Ma Carrico's Buttermilk Pancakes

Sheila Cope
Colorado Springs, CO

These pancakes are the best! I got this recipe from Irene Carrico, who has since passed away, while I was working for her at the Arctic Circle Restaurant in Kanab, Utah. "Ma" made these for me every morning... sometimes she would spoil me by adding mashed bananas to the batter and drizzling strawberry syrup over the top.

1 c. all-purpose flour	1 c. buttermilk
1 t. baking powder	1 egg, beaten
1/4 t. baking soda	3 T. sugar
1/2 t. salt	3 T. oil

Combine all ingredients; mix well. Pour by 1/4 cupfuls on a hot griddle sprayed with non-stick vegetable spray over medium heat. Cook pancakes until golden and bubbles appear around edges; flip and cook other side. Makes 12 to 15, 4-inch pancakes.

Homemade pancakes on a weekday morning...what a treat! Pancakes can be stored in plastic freezer bags for up to a month. To serve, place pancakes in a single layer on a baking sheet, cover with aluminum foil and bake at 350 degrees for about 10 minutes. Please pass the syrup!

Marine Corps Breakfast

Marilyn Miller
Fort Washington, PA

From my dad's days in the U.S. Marine Corps...anyone with a hearty appetite will appreciate this old favorite!

1/2 lb. ground beef
1 T. bacon drippings
1/8 t. salt
3 T. all-purpose flour

2 c. milk
salt and pepper to taste
8 slices white bread, toasted

In a large skillet over medium heat, brown and crumble ground beef with drippings and salt. Remove skillet from heat; let cool slightly. Mix in flour until all of the beef is covered. Return skillet to medium heat and stir in milk. Cook and stir until mixture comes to a boil and thickens; boil for at least one minute. Serve over toast. Serves 2 hungry Marines or 8 regular diners.

Red-Eye Gravy & Biscuits

Stacie Avner
Gooseberry Patch

My grandma lived in Kentucky and whenever we visited her, my dad would pick up a country ham to bring home. This was my favorite breakfast that my dad made for us on chilly mornings.

2 T. butter
6 slices country-style ham
1 T. all-purpose flour
1 c. strong brewed coffee
1-1/2 T. brown sugar, packed

1/2 c. water
salt and pepper to taste
Optional: hot pepper sauce to
  taste
6 biscuits, split and buttered

Melt butter in a skillet over medium-high heat. Cook ham slices until lightly browned; remove from skillet. Add flour to drippings in skillet; cook and stir for one minute. Add coffee, brown sugar and water. Cook and stir for 3 minutes, until thickened; return ham to skillet. Stir in seasonings. Serve ham and gravy over biscuits. Serves 6.

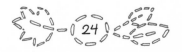

Farm-Fresh *Breakfasts*

Sausage & Cheddar Grits

Sharon Brown
Orange Park, FL

A rich, savory version of a southern favorite...yum!

4 c. water
1 t. salt
1 c. quick-cooking grits,
   uncooked
4 eggs, beaten
1 lb. ground pork sausage,
   browned and drained

1-1/2 c. shredded Cheddar
   cheese, divided
1 c. milk
1/4 c. butter

Bring water and salt to boil in a large saucepan over medium heat. Stir in grits; cook for 4 to 5 minutes. Remove from heat. Stir a small amount of hot grits mixture into eggs; stir egg mixture into saucepan. Add sausage, one cup cheese, milk and butter; blend together well. Pour into a greased 13"x9" baking pan. Sprinkle with remaining cheese. Bake, uncovered, at 350 degrees for one hour, or until cheese is golden. If cheese is getting golden early, cover with aluminum foil. Let cool for about 10 minutes before serving. Serves 6 to 8.

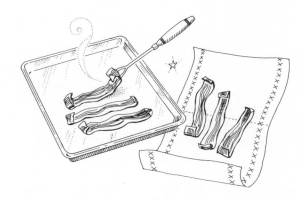

A quick, no-mess way to cook bacon. Arrange bacon slices on a broiler pan and place the pan 3 to 4 inches from the preheated broiler. Broil for one to 2 minutes on each side, depending on how crispy you like your bacon.

Just Peachy French Toast

Vickie

Top with a dollop of whipped cream...scrumptious!

1 c. brown sugar, packed
1/2 c. butter
2 T. water
29-oz. can sliced peaches,
   drained

12 slices day-old French bread
5 eggs, beaten
1 T. vanilla extract
cinnamon to taste
Garnish: maple syrup

The night before, combine brown sugar, butter and water in a saucepan; bring to a boil. Reduce heat to low; cook for 10 minutes, stirring frequently. Pour into a greased 13"x9" baking pan, tilting to coat bottom of pan. Arrange peaches in pan; top with bread and set aside. Whisk together eggs and vanilla; pour over bread to coat evenly. Sprinkle with cinnamon. Cover and refrigerate overnight. In the morning, let stand at room temperature for 30 minutes. Uncover and bake at 350 degrees for 25 to 30 minutes, until golden. Serve with syrup. Makes 8 servings.

Marlene's Pancake Syrup

Beth Bundy
Long Prairie, MN

*This recipe was created by my mother many years ago...
it brings back warm, sticky memories!*

2 c. sugar
1 c. brown sugar, packed
1-1/2 c. water

2 T. corn syrup
1 t. maple flavoring

In a medium saucepan over medium heat, stir together all ingredients except maple flavoring. Simmer for 5 minutes; add flavoring. Stir to combine and serve. Refrigerate any leftovers. Makes 3 cups.

*For a change, try an old farmhouse tradition...a big slice
of apple or cherry pie for breakfast!*

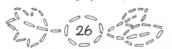

Farm-Fresh *Breakfasts*

Trudy's Cherry Coffee Cake

Dawn Menard
Seekonk, MA

This was given to me by my friend Kelley...it's a recipe from her mother Trudy. I like to make it with different fruit fillings like blueberry or apple and various nuts like pecans or almonds. My son requests it often!

1 egg, beaten	21-oz. can cherry pie filling,
1/4 c. milk	partially drained
1/2 c. sugar	1/2 c. brown sugar, packed
1/8 t. salt	1/2 t. cinnamon
1/2 t. vanilla extract	3 T. butter, diced
1-3/4 c. biscuit baking mix,	1/3 c. chopped walnuts
divided	

Combine egg, milk, sugar, salt, vanilla and 1-1/2 cups baking mix. Stir until smooth. Pour mixture into a lightly greased 8"x8" baking pan. Spoon pie filling over mixture in pan. Mix together remaining baking mix, brown sugar, cinnamon, butter and nuts. Sprinkle over pie filling. Bake at 375 degrees for 30 minutes. Cut into squares. Makes 6 to 8 servings.

Looking for a new family message board? Hang an old-fashioned washboard for a whimsical way to keep notes organized. Just use magnets to keep messages and photos secure.

Walnut-Maple Streusel Cake

Sarah Oravecz
Gooseberry Patch

*A delectable sweet treat any time of day! This cake keeps well,
so feel free to bake it the day before and store it,
wrapped in plastic, at room temperature.*

2 c. all-purpose flour
1 t. baking powder
1 t. baking soda
1/2 t. salt
3/4 c. sugar

1/2 c. butter, room temperature
2 eggs, beaten
1 t. vanilla extract
8-oz. container sour cream

Whisk together flour, baking powder, baking soda and salt in a medium bowl; set aside. In a large bowl, with an electric mixer on medium-high speed, beat sugar and butter until fluffy. Beat in eggs and vanilla. Beat in flour mixture alternately with sour cream, mixing just until blended. Spoon half of batter into a buttered and floured Bundt® pan. Spoon 2/3 of Walnut Filling over batter. Spread remaining batter over filling; smooth top. Dot with remaining filling. Bake at 350 degrees for 40 minutes, until a toothpick inserted near center tests done. Cool cake in pan on a wire rack for 15 minutes. Run a knife around pan sides to loosen; turn cake out onto a serving platter. Serves 12.

Walnut Filling:

1/2 c. all-purpose flour
2 T. butter, softened
1 t. cinnamon

1-1/4 c. chopped walnuts
1/2 c. maple syrup

With a fork, mix together flour, butter and cinnamon in a small bowl until crumbly. Stir in nuts and syrup.

*A vintage hand-cranked mini food chopper makes short
work of chopping nuts for cakes, cookies and other recipes.*

Farm-Fresh *Breakfasts*

Niles Coffee Cake

Dawn Wright
Marysville, OH

I had a dear elderly lady friend, Martha, who rented me a room when I was younger. She would make this most delicious coffee cake and we couldn't keep out of it. She always called it "Niles Coffee Cake" after the church she attended in Niles, Michigan. I loved her dearly and I always think of her when I make this coffee cake.

1 loaf frozen bread dough
1 c. chopped pecans or walnuts
1/2 c. cook & serve butterscotch
   pudding mix

1/2 c. butter
1/2 c. brown sugar, packed

The night before, let frozen bread dough stand at room temperature for one hour. Cut dough into 16 pieces and roll into balls. Spray a Bundt® pan with non-stick vegetable spray; sprinkle nuts into bottom of pan. Arrange dough balls in pan; sprinkle with pudding mix and set aside. In a small saucepan over medium-high heat, melt butter and brown sugar together. Pour hot mixture over dough balls. Cover pan; let rise overnight at room temperature. In the morning, bake at 325 degrees for 25 to 30 minutes, until rolls are light golden. Turn out onto a decorative plate; serve warm. Serves 6 to 8.

A weekend morning is the perfect time for an old-fashioned kaffeeklatsch to chat over coffee cake and coffee. Invite a girlfriend, or the new neighbor you've been wanting to get to know better, to share the latest news...you'll be so glad you did!

Mary Ann's Sunrise Egg Bake

Kathy Grashoff
Fort Wayne, IN

This is my absolute go-to egg casserole...it is so good! It's my mother-in-law's recipe and I have been using it for over 30 years. You should see my poor recipe card...you can tell it's a favorite! I always make a couple of all-vegetable bakes, too...try adding onions, colorful red and green peppers and whatever else you like.

1 doz. eggs, beaten
1 c. evaporated milk
2 t. dry mustard
salt and pepper to taste
8-oz. pkg. shredded Cheddar
   cheese

1 c. cooked ham, chopped
8-oz. can sliced mushrooms,
   drained
1/4 c. butter, diced

In a large bowl, whisk eggs, milk, mustard, salt and pepper together. Stir in cheese, ham and mushrooms. Pour into a lightly greased 13"x9" baking pan; dot with butter. Bake, uncovered, at 300 degrees for 45 minutes. Cool slightly before slicing into squares. Makes 12 servings.

Serve up individual portions of breakfast eggs in retro pressed-glass "hen-on-a-nest" dishes. The chicken-shaped lids will keep food hot and tasty, with a dash of fun added!

Farm-Fresh *Breakfasts*

Golden Hashbrown Casserole

Renae Scheiderer
Beallsville, OH

A wonderful recipe to make when you have company coming...
just pop it in the oven and let it bake while you visit!

6 eggs, beaten
12-oz. can evaporated milk
1 t. salt
1/2 t. pepper
30-oz. pkg. frozen shredded
   hashbrowns

8-oz. pkg. shredded Cheddar
   cheese
1 onion, chopped
1 green pepper, chopped
1 c. cooked ham, diced

Whisk eggs, milk, salt and pepper in a large bowl. Add remaining
ingredients; mix well. Pour mixture into a greased 13"x9" baking pan.
Bake, uncovered, at 350 degrees for 60 to 65 minutes, or until eggs
are set. Makes 10 to 12 servings.

Make your own country-style sausage patties...it's simple.
To one pound ground pork, add one teaspoon ground sage,
3/4 teaspoon salt, 3/4 teaspoon pepper and 1/4 teaspoon
brown sugar. A dash or two of cayenne pepper can be
added too. Blend well, form into four patties and
brown in a skillet...delicious!

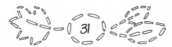

Custardy French Toast

Sarah Cameron
Maryville, TN

Absolutely the best French toast you'll ever eat!

6 eggs, beaten
3/4 c. whipping cream
3/4 c. milk
1/4 c. sugar
1/4 t. cinnamon

1 loaf French bread, thickly
  sliced
2 T. butter, divided
Optional: powdered sugar

In a large shallow bowl, whisk eggs, cream, milk, sugar and cinnamon until well blended. Dip bread slices one at a time into egg mixture, turning to allow both sides to absorb mixture. Melt one tablespoon butter on a non-stick griddle over medium heat. Cook for about 4 minutes per side, until golden and firm to the touch. Repeat with remaining butter and bread. Dust with powdered sugar, if desired. Serve with warm Cinnamon Syrup. Serves 6 to 8.

Cinnamon Syrup:

1 c. water
1 c. dark brown sugar, packed

2 T. whipping cream
1/2 t. cinnamon

Combine water and brown sugar in a heavy saucepan. Bring to a boil over high heat, stirring until sugar dissolves. Boil until syrup reduces to one cup, about 10 minutes. Remove from heat; whisk in cream and cinnamon. Serve warm. Syrup may be refrigerated, then rewarmed at serving time. Makes about 2 cups.

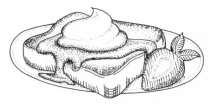

*Keep tea towels handy on a peg rack...stitch a folded loop
of rick rack to one corner of the towels for hanging.*

Picnic
in the Country

Hearty Hoagie

Jo Ann

*We love to grill these sandwiches practically year 'round in our
backyard fire ring. You can also slide the foil-wrapped sandwich
onto a baking sheet and bake it at 350 degrees until hot.*

2 T. olive oil
1 T. white wine vinegar
1/3 c. fresh basil, chopped
1 loaf French bread, halved
   lengthwise

6-oz. pkg. sliced mozzarella
   cheese, divided
6-oz. pkg. sliced pastrami
2 roma tomatoes, thinly sliced
pepper to taste

Whisk together oil, vinegar and basil in a small bowl; set aside.
Hollow out bottom half of loaf, leaving a 1/2-inch thick shell. Layer
with half of cheese, all of the pastrami and tomatoes. Drizzle with oil
mixture; sprinkle with pepper. Layer with remaining cheese; add top
half of loaf. Wrap in aluminum foil. Grill over medium heat for 20 to
25 minutes, turning every 5 minutes, until heated through. Slice
crosswise to serve. Makes 4 to 6 servings.

*Fill an old wooden sugar bucket with crushed ice and bottles
of soda pop...everyone can help themselves to a frosty beverage.*

Picnic in the Country

Farmhands' Stuffed Sandwich

Barbara Shultis
South Egremont, MA

You'll love this oversized sandwich...wrapped in plastic, it's perfect for carrying to a picnic. I've done SO many tasty variations on this sandwich...chicken with barbecue sauce, ham & Swiss with coleslaw, corned beef & sauerkraut with Thousand Island dressing. The mix & match possibilities are endless!

1 round loaf hearty bread
2 T. Italian salad dressing
8 slices provolone cheese, divided
1/8 lb. deli salami, sliced
2-1/4 oz. can sliced black olives, drained
1/2 lb. mild Italian pork sausage links, browned and sliced

1 thick slice red onion
6 T. pizza sauce
6 pepperoncini, drained and sliced
1/4 lb. deli turkey, sliced
4-oz. jar sun-dried tomatoes in oil, drained and sliced
2 T. grated Parmesan cheese
Optional: 2 T. garlic, pressed

Slice off top quarter of loaf; hollow out top and bottom of loaf. Brush salad dressing inside bottom half. Layer with half of cheese slices; layer on remaining ingredients in order listed, ending with remaining cheese slices. Replace top half of loaf. Place on a baking sheet; set another baking sheet on top. Weight down with a heavy object like a food can or a cast-iron skillet. Let stand for 30 minutes to one hour. Cut into wedges to serve. Makes 10 servings.

Wicker picnic baskets just like Mom's are easy to find at tag sales... they bring back fond childhood memories of picnic fun! When yours isn't being used to tote picnic goodies, keep it in the kitchen to hold a collection of favorite cookbooks.

Egg Salad Sandwiches

Jenni Staroscik
Castle Rock, CO

Try replacing some of the onion with snipped fresh chives...delightful!

6 eggs, hard-boiled, peeled and
   coarsely chopped
1/2 c. shredded Cheddar cheese
1 onion, finely chopped
2/3 c. mayonnaise
1 t. mustard

1/4 t. paprika
1/4 t. celery salt
1/4 t. salt
1/4 t. pepper
8 slices bread, toasted

Mix all ingredients together except bread. Cover and refrigerate until serving time. Serve on toasted bread. Makes 4 sandwiches.

Mix up some herbal vinegar. Fill a Mason jar with a cup of finely chopped fresh herbs like parsley, chives, basil and dill. Pour in 2 cups white wine vinegar, heated just to boiling. Cap the jar and let steep, shaking it gently now and then. Strain the vinegar after 3 weeks and use it to jazz up salads and deli sandwiches.

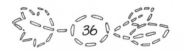

Picnic in the Country

Picnic Salad Skewers

Pam James
Gooseberry Patch

What a fun way to pack a salad! For a meal-in-one version,
slide on some cubes of Cheddar cheese and cold cuts too.

8 new redskin potatoes
8 pearl onions
1 green pepper, cut into 1-inch
   squares
1 red or yellow pepper, cut into
   1-inch squares

16 cherry tomatoes
1 zucchini, sliced 1/4-inch thick
8 wooden skewers
Optional: 4-oz. container
   crumbled feta cheese

Cover potatoes with water in a saucepan; bring to a boil over medium heat. Cook for 10 to 13 minutes, adding onions after 5 minutes; drain and cool. Thread vegetables alternately onto skewers. Arrange skewers in a large shallow plastic container. Drizzle with vinaigrette. Cover and refrigerate for at least one hour, turning frequently. Sprinkle with cheese before serving, if desired. Makes 8 servings.

Vinaigrette:

2/3 c. olive oil
1/3 c. red wine vinegar
2 cloves garlic, minced

1 T. dried oregano
1 t. salt
1/4 t. pepper

Whisk all ingredients together.

A rustic metal watering can
makes a charming centerpiece
filled with stems of cutting-garden
favorites like silver dollar plant,
Chinese lanterns and bells of Ireland.

Mom's Strawberry Lemonade

Kathleen Sturm
Corona, CA

*Here in southern California, we're lucky to have a lemon tree in
our backyard. This refreshing thirst quencher is a staple
in our fridge during the hot summer months.*

2 c. lemon juice
2 c. sugar

1 c. strawberries, hulled and
   puréed

In a one-gallon jug or pitcher, combine lemon juice, sugar and puréed
strawberries. Mix to start dissolving sugar. Add enough water to fill
jug. Stir until sugar is dissolved completely. Chill; serve ice-cold.
Makes one gallon.

Homemade Root Beer

Beth Bundy
Long Prairie, MN

A tried & true recipe that will really take you back in time.

3/4 c. water
1/4 t. vanilla extract
1/2 c. sugar
1/4 c. honey

1/2 t. plus 1/8 t. root beer
   concentrate
4-1/4 c. carbonated water or
   club soda

Combine water and vanilla in a saucepan. Heat over low heat until
steaming. Remove from heat. Add sugar and honey; stir until
dissolved. Add concentrate. Mix well and cool in refrigerator. When
chilled, slowly add carbonated water or club soda. Serve immediately.
Makes about 6 servings.

When fate hands you a lemon, make lemonade.
-Dale Carnegie

Picnic in the Country

Pineapple Cheese Ball

Michelle Campen
Peoria, IL

Tote along one of these yummy cheese balls in a mini cooler with a box of crisp crackers to munch on after a hike in the country.

8-oz. pkg. cream cheese,
  softened
2 c. chopped pecans, divided
1/4 c. green pepper, chopped

8-oz. can crushed pineapple,
  drained
2 T. onion, chopped
1 T. seasoned salt

Beat cream cheese until smooth. Blend in one cup pecans and remaining ingredients. Shape into a ball; roll in remaining pecans. Wrap in plastic wrap. Refrigerate until ready to serve. Makes one cheese ball.

Box lunches are a fun way to serve up a picnic...indoors or out!
Decorate shoeboxes with scrapbooking paper, stickers,
ribbons and bows. Tuck a sandwich, a shiny red apple,
some cookies and a napkin into each box.

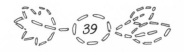

Tuna & Egg Salad Sandwiches

Kimberly Stine
Milford, PA

Not your ordinary tuna salad sandwich! Only the egg whites are used...
chop the hard-cooked yolks to sprinkle over a salad.

2 6-oz. cans white tuna,
   drained and flaked
1/4 c. celery, minced
2 T. onion, minced
salt and pepper to taste
2 eggs, hard-boiled, peeled and
   halved

1/3 c. mayonnaise
8 slices Italian bread
Garnish: lettuce leaves, tomato
   slices, pickles

In a large bowl, combine tuna, celery, onion, salt and pepper to taste. Chop egg whites and add to mixture, setting aside yolks for another recipe. Mix well and add mayonnaise until desired consistency. Serve on bread, garnished as desired with lettuce, tomatoes and pickles. Makes 4 sandwiches.

The next time you see a roadside stand in the country, stop and take a look! You're sure to find the freshest fruits & veggies, cut flowers and even homemade goodies like pickles, preserves, pies and cakes.

Picnic in the Country

Almost Heaven Chicken Salad

Pamela Breesawitz
White Sulphur Springs, WV

This chicken salad is a local favorite. My mother would often make it to take along on Sunday picnics as a light lunch. Even though she is no longer with us, I still make this recipe for my family...everyone loves it!

1/2 T. lemon juice
3 lbs. chicken breast, cooked
   and cubed
3/4 c. celery, finely diced

1/2 c. onion, finely chopped
1 c. mayonnaise
1 c. sour cream
salt and pepper to taste

Sprinkle lemon juice over chicken in a large bowl. Add remaining ingredients; mix well. Cover and chill well. May be served as a luncheon salad or on sandwiches. Makes 10 to 15 servings.

It's easy to tote a salad to a picnic. Mix it up in a plastic zipping bag, seal and set it right in the cooler. When you arrive at the picnic grounds, simply tip the salad into a serving bowl.

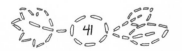

Ham & Pickle Roll-Ups

Kristi Ohler
Rockwood, PA

*When I take these roll-ups to a family get-together, they are gone
before we even sit down to eat dinner! They are very tasty
and so easy to make.*

8-oz. pkg. cream cheese,
  softened
1 lb. deli ham, thinly sliced

32-oz. jar dill pickle spears,
  drained

Spread cream cheese on ham slices. Lay a pickle at the edge of each
ham slice and roll up. Push a toothpick through it to hold it together.
Slice into pieces the size you prefer. Store roll-ups in an airtight
container; keep refrigerated. Makes 2 to 3 dozen.

*Keep picnic food cold...fill plastic bottles with homemade
lemonade or iced tea, freeze and tuck into your picnic cooler.
As the bottles thaw, you'll have refreshing beverages to enjoy too.*

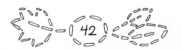

Picnic in the Country

Horseradish Deviled Eggs

Karen McCann
Marion, OH

I remember when my mother first made these deviled eggs. She just chuckled as we tried to guess what was in them...horseradish! It gives the eggs a mild but zesty flavor.

6 eggs, hard-boiled, peeled and
    halved lengthwise
1/4 c. mayonnaise
1 to 2 T. prepared horseradish
1/4 t. mustard

1/8 t. salt
1/8 t. pepper
Optional: 1/2 t. dill weed
Garnish: paprika

Scoop egg yolks into a bowl. Arrange egg white halves on a platter and set aside. Mash yolks with a fork. Add mayonnaise, horseradish to taste, mustard, salt, pepper and dill weed, if using; mix well. Spoon mixture into egg whites; sprinkle with paprika. Refrigerate until ready to serve. Makes 12 servings.

Toting deviled eggs to a carry-in? Nestle the eggs in a bed of shredded lettuce or curly parsley to keep them from sliding around...they'll arrive looking scrumptious!

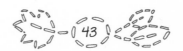

Chicken Noodle Burgers

Judy Borecky
Escondido, CA

This recipe is from my mother. She lived to see her great-great-grandchildren and her 100th birthday, bless her heart. Mother loved to cook and all 5 generations of our family love her noodle burgers!

1-1/4 lbs. ground beef round
10-3/4 oz. can chicken noodle
   soup, drained
1/3 c. instant oats, uncooked
1 egg, beaten
onion salt and pepper to taste
1/2 lb. sliced mushrooms

1/4 c. butter
3 T. all-purpose flour
1 c. chicken broth
1 c. half-and-half
1 t. Dijon mustard
salt and pepper to taste

Combine ground beef, soup, oats, egg, onion salt and pepper. Mix all until just blended and form into 6 patties. Place patties in a skillet over medium-high heat. Add a little water to the skillet so patties will steam as they fry. Meanwhile, make gravy in a separate skillet. Sauté mushrooms in butter until tender. Stir in flour, broth and half-and-half; cook until slightly thickened. Stir in mustard; add salt and pepper to taste. Serve gravy over noodle burgers. Makes 6 servings.

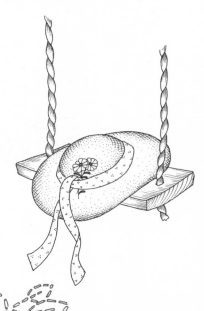

Hang a collection of fanciful
straw hats on a rack
by the kitchen door, just
waiting for a trip into
town or a few minutes
in the garden.

Picnic in the Country

Farm Sale Barbecue

Mardell Ross
Genoa, IL

*These delicious sandwiches are a family tradition after we watch
the parade at the local pumpkin festival.*

2 lbs. ground beef
2 onions, chopped
10-3/4 oz. can tomato soup
3 T. catsup

1 T. dry mustard
1 T. vinegar
8 to 10 hamburger buns, split

In a large skillet over medium heat, brown ground beef and onions
together; drain. Add soup, catsup, mustard and vinegar. Let simmer
for 10 minutes or more. Serve spooned onto buns. Serves 8 to 10.

No picnic table? No problem! Lay a length of plywood
(or even an old door) across a couple of sawhorses and
toss on a checkered tablecloth. Add straw bales for
seating and you're ready for a farm-style picnic!

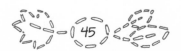

Ham-Stuffed Tiny Tomatoes

Holly Curry
Grahamsville, NY

A recipe given to me at a church supper...it is so very good!
Use a tiny measuring spoon to scoop out the tomatoes.

1 pt. cherry tomatoes
4-1/2 oz. can deviled ham
   spread

2 T. sour cream
2 T. horseradish sauce
Garnish: chopped fresh parsley

Slice tops off tomatoes and scoop out pulp. Place tomatoes upside-down on paper towels to drain. In a small bowl, mix remaining ingredients except parsley. Spoon or pipe ham mixture into tomatoes; sprinkle with parsley. Chill. Makes about 20 servings.

Brightly colored bandannas are fun to use as super-sized
napkins. Keep a stack of them on hand and you'll be
ready for a picnic or casual get-together anytime.

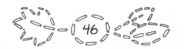

Picnic in the Country

Mini Bacon-Cheese Balls

Ruby Dorosh
Shippensburg, PA

*These tasty bite-size appetizers are sure to be a hit at
your next picnic, potluck or pitch-in dinner!*

8-oz. container chive & onion
   cream cheese spread,
   softened
8-oz. pkg. shredded mozzarella
   cheese
4 slices bacon, crisply cooked
   and crumbled

1/2 t. Italian seasoning
1/2 t. garlic powder
1/2 c. walnuts, toasted and
   ground or finely chopped

Mix cheeses until well blended; stir in bacon and seasonings. Shape
mixture into balls by level teaspoonfuls. Roll each ball in walnuts.
Place in a serving dish; cover with plastic wrap. Refrigerate at least
2 hours before serving. Makes about 4-1/2 dozen.

*A fluffy chenille bedspread that has become a little shabby is
just right for a picnic spread. Tuck one in your car and
you'll be ready for picnicking at a moment's notice.*

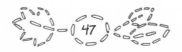

Wiener Kabobs

Clarie Bertram
Lexington, KY

*My brother & I always felt so grown-up when Mom served these
appetizers. Of course we had to take off the olives and stick
them on our fingers...maybe that's why we liked them so much!*

1-lb. pkg. mini cocktail wieners
11-oz. can pineapple chunks,
   drained
5-oz. jar green olives with
   pimentos, drained

1/2 lb. favorite cheese, cubed
party picks or mini wooden
   skewers

Place one wiener, one pineapple chunk, one olive and one cheese
cube on each pick or skewer. Repeat until ingredients are used up.
Arrange picks on a serving plate and cover with plastic wrap. Keep
chilled until ready to serve. Makes 2 to 3 dozen.

Retro plastic catsup & mustard squeeze bottles
add a little fun to any meal.

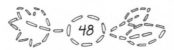

Picnic in the Country

Corn Relish Dip

Dianne Young
South Jordan, UT

This is a real crowd-pleaser...everyone always asks for the recipe.
Serve with tortilla chips for dipping or spoon into lettuce cups
and serve as a salad. Either way, it's yummy!

3 roma tomatoes, diced
2 avocados, pitted, peeled and
  diced
15-oz. can shoepeg corn,
  drained
16-oz. can black beans, drained
  and rinsed

3.8-oz. can sliced black olives,
  drained
1/4 to 1/2 c. onion, diced
16-oz. bottle zesty Italian salad
  dressing

Combine all vegetables in a large salad bowl; toss to mix. Add
dressing to taste, a little at a time. Keep chilled; stir again before
serving. Makes 8 servings.

Keep tea towels at your fingertips on the counter by the
kitchen sink. Slip rolled-up towels into a
vintage milk bottle carrier.

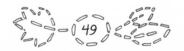

Aunt Janie's Famous Cheese Ball

Wendy O'Hara-Reaume
Ontario, Canada

This recipe has been a part of our family gatherings for as long as I can remember. With its savory combination of flavors, it's always a big hit at parties...maybe you'd better double the recipe!

2 8-oz. pkgs. cream cheese, softened
4-oz. container crumbled blue cheese
1 c. shredded Cheddar cheese
1 green pepper, diced
2-oz. jar diced pimentos, drained
1 t. Worcestershire sauce
1 t. garlic powder
1 c. sliced almonds
round buttery crackers or club crackers

Combine all ingredients except almonds and crackers; blend well. Form into one or two balls. Place almonds into a lidded plastic container. Place cheese ball into container (one at a time, if making two) and cover with lid. Shake vigorously to coat with nuts. Wrap and refrigerate until serving time. Serve with crackers. Makes 10 to 12 servings.

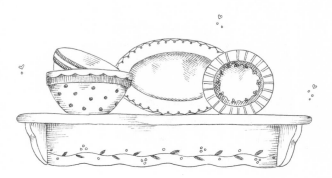

Show off a collection of favorite stoneware mixing bowls on open-front kitchen shelves. Add a pretty shelf edging of scrapbooking paper, trimmed with decorative-edge scissors.

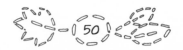

Picnic in the Country

Nutty Olive Spread

Hope Davenport
Portland, TX

Tuck a jar of this creamy spread, a cheese spreader and some crisp crackers into a basket for a neighborly gift that's sure to be welcome.

2 3-oz. pkgs. cream cheese, softened
1/2 c. mayonnaise
5-3/4 oz. jar green olives with pimentos, drained and finely chopped

1/2 c. pecans, toasted and finely chopped
1/8 t. pepper
assorted crackers

In a large bowl, beat cream cheese until fluffy; beat in mayonnaise. Stir in olives, pecans and pepper. Cover and chill overnight. Serve with crackers. Makes about 2 cups.

Keep the fridge sweet-smelling...tuck in a cotton ball that has been moistened with vanilla extract. A little trick that works with picnic coolers too.

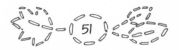

Gallon Jug Pineapple Punch

Audrey Musick
Marion, VA

My mother always kept a big jug of this punch in the fridge...
she had a hard time keeping us kids out of the jug!

26-oz. can pineapple juice
2 qts. cold water
1 c. sugar

2 .17-oz. pkgs. unsweetened
  lemon-lime drink mix
1 qt. ginger ale, chilled

Mix together pineapple juice, water, sugar and drink mix in a one-gallon jug or pitcher. Stir until sugar is well dissolved. Chill until ready to serve. Just before serving, add ginger ale. Makes one gallon.

Keep buzzing bees out of picnic beverages. Just stitch 4 large buttons from Grandma's button box to a large doily and drape it over an open pitcher...it's that easy!

Picnic in the Country

Picnic Fruit Punch

Beth Bundy
Long Prairie, MN

Oh-so refreshing on a summer day.

2 qts. cranberry juice cocktail
3 c. pineapple juice
3 c. orange juice

1/4 c. lemon juice
1 ltr. ginger ale, chilled
Garnish: 1 orange, thinly sliced

Combine the juices together in a very large pitcher. Refrigerate for one hour or longer. Just before serving, stir in ginger ale; garnish with orange slices. Makes slightly over one gallon.

A sweet vintage-style clothespin bag makes a handy wall holder for recipe cards or mail.

Country Bologna Salad

Karen Smyers
Yadkinville, NC

This is my mother's recipe...it was handed down from her mother, my Grandmother Startzell, so it is quite old. The hard-boiled eggs are my own addition.

3 lbs. beef bologna, coarsely
   chopped
16-oz. jar sweet pickles, drained
2 eggs, hard-boiled, peeled and
   chopped

1 to 1-1/2 c. mayonnaise-style
   salad dressing

Grind bologna and pickles in a food grinder to desired medium to coarse texture. Transfer to a large bowl; add eggs. Stir in salad dressing to desired consistency. Blend ingredients together. Spread on bread for sandwiches or on crackers for appetizers. Makes 15 to 20 servings.

An old-fashioned food grinder is easy to clean when you've finished using it. Just put a half-slice of bread through the grinder as the last item...the bread will remove any food residue.

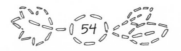

Picnic in the Country

Picnic Pinwheels

Kimberly Hancock
Murrieta, CA

These roll-ups are lots of fun for kids, and moms as well, because they can be made in just minutes. It's a great spin on our old standby, the peanut butter & jelly sandwich. Crunchy apple can be substituted for the banana too. Yummy!

1/3 c. creamy peanut butter	1 c. banana, chopped
4 8-inch flour tortillas	1/4 c. low-fat granola cereal

Spread peanut butter on each tortilla; top with banana and granola. Tightly roll up tortillas and cut each one in half. Wrap roll-ups in plastic wrap or aluminum foil to pack in lunchboxes. Serves 4.

Instead of one large picnic basket, why not pack individual lunches for everyone in children's sand pails? Line the pails with checked napkins and tie a name tag to the handle of each pail.

Spicy Cheese Crispies

Molly Wilson
Box Elder, SD

*All the kids loved the regular mild-flavored cheese crispies and my
uncle told Mama she should make some for the adults...so she did!*

1 c. margarine, softened
8-oz. pkg. shredded sharp
   Cheddar cheese
2 c. all-purpose flour

1 t. cayenne pepper
1/2 t. salt
2 c. crispy rice cereal
Optional: 1 c. pecan halves

In a large bowl, blend together margarine and cheese. Add flour,
cayenne pepper and salt; stir in cereal. Shape into small balls and
place on ungreased baking sheets. Flatten each ball with a fork.
Top each with a pecan half, if desired. Bake at 300 degrees for
20 minutes. Cool; store tightly covered. Makes about 6 dozen.

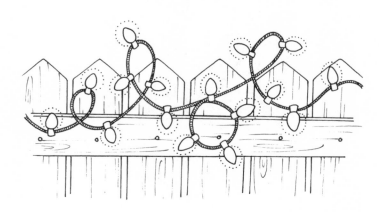

*Wind sparkling yellow or white lights along the garden fence
and in the trees for a twinkling firefly effect as the sun sets.*

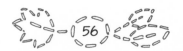

Picnic in the Country

Tasty Taco Roll-Ups

*Kelly Bartle-Gardner
Central Square, NY*

*Sprinkle on some finely chopped red and green pepper
for extra color and crunchiness.*

3 8-oz. pkgs. cream cheese
1/2 c. shredded Cheddar cheese
1-1/4 oz. pkg. taco seasoning
   mix

10 to 12 10-inch flour tortillas
Garnish: salsa

Stir together cheeses and seasoning mix until well blended. Spread evenly onto tortillas; roll up tightly. Cut rolls into bite-size pieces; chill. Serve with salsa for dipping. Makes about 5 to 6 dozen.

*Vintage tin pie plates are practical for holding picnic dinners...
not flimsy like paper plates! Look for tins that are stamped
with the names of the original bakeries.*

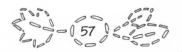

Sour Cream Dill Dip

Frankie Barnette
Colonial Heights, VA

This dip recipe brings back so many memories of my grandmother! My brother and I were always asking our "Gaga" to make it for us when we were little. We just loved eating it with ruffled potato chips or toasted bread pieces. Now that she has passed on, I'm the one who always makes this great dip.

1 c. sour cream	1 t. seasoning salt
2/3 c. mayonnaise	1 t. dried, minced onion
1-1/2 t. dill weed	potato chips, cut-up veggies

Mix all ingredients together except potato chips and vegetables. Cover and refrigerate for one to 2 hours, until dip becomes firm. Serve with chips and vegetables for dipping. Makes 12 to 15 servings.

Baby carrots, celery stalks, cherry tomatoes and broccoli flowerets are all tasty dippers...why not try something new with your next bowl of dip? Slices of yellow summer squash, romaine lettuce leaves and even lightly steamed green beans, snow peas and asparagus spears are crunchy and full of flavor.

Picnic in the Country

Cheesy Bean Dip

Diana Seiler
Goddard, KS

This dip is a favorite at our family get-togethers like picnics,
football games or just Sunday night gatherings.

2 16-oz. cans refried beans
2 8-oz. pkgs. cream cheese,
    softened
Garnish: shredded Cheddar or
    Swiss cheese, chopped green
    onions

tortilla chips, snack crackers

Spoon beans into a large bowl. Slowly blend in cream cheese until creamy, using an electric mixer set on medium-low speed. Garnish as desired with cheese and onions. Chill before serving with chips or crackers. Serves 6 to 8.

Primitive-style wooden cutting boards in fun shapes like pigs,
fish or roosters can often be found at tag sales. Put them
to use as whimsical party snack servers.

Zesty Tortilla Roll-Ups

Rosemary Vorndran
Diamond Bar, CA

*We always share several kinds of finger foods like these roll-ups
before the main meal at family get-togethers. It gives us a
chance to mingle, chat and catch up with each other.*

2 8-oz. pkgs. cream cheese,
  softened
2 4-oz. cans chopped green
  chiles, drained

2 to 3 T. milk
10 to 12 burrito-size flour
  tortillas

In a medium bowl, mix cream cheese and chiles with enough milk to
make smooth and easy to spread. Spread mixture on tortillas and roll
up tightly. Slice rolled-up tortillas in one-inch pieces and arrange on a
serving plate. May be made the day before, chilled and sliced when
ready to serve. Makes about 1-1/2 dozen.

*Straw shopping totes from the thrift store make whimsical
planters for marigolds and zinnias...just slip them
over fence posts and fill with flowers.*

Garden-Fresh
Salads
& Sides

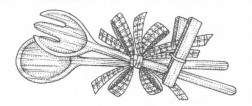

Garden-Fresh Green Beans

Vickie Fallis
Osgood, IN

This recipe came from a cookbook from the 1940's. It's such a treat made with the first green beans, peppers and tomatoes of the season.

4 to 6 slices smoked bacon,
   diced
2 lbs. green beans, trimmed
1 onion, diced

1 green pepper, diced
1 tomato, diced
salt and pepper to taste

In a large heavy skillet over medium heat, cook bacon until crisp. Set aside bacon, reserving drippings in skillet. Add remaining ingredients to skillet. Cover tightly and reduce heat; cook for 10 minutes. Add just enough water to cover bottom of skillet; increase heat and cook until beans are tender. Stir in cooked bacon. Serves 8.

I have friends in overalls whose friendship I would not swap for the favor of the kings of the world.
-Thomas Edison

Garden-Fresh Salads & Sides

Creamy Country Corn

Sharon Demers
Dolores, CO

*This easy recipe is a tasty accompaniment to grilled meat
and a crisp green tossed salad.*

6 green onions, chopped
3 T. butter
16-oz. pkg. frozen corn, thawed
2 t. cornstarch
1/2 c. half-and-half

1/4 c. water
1/2 t. salt
1/4 to 1/2 t. pepper
1 c. cherry tomatoes, halved

In a skillet over medium heat, sauté onions in butter until tender, about 2 to 3 minutes. Stir in corn; cover and cook until heated through, about 4 to 5 minutes. In a small bowl, combine cornstarch, half-and-half, water, salt and pepper; whisk until smooth. Stir into corn mixture. Bring to a boil. Cook, uncovered, until thickened, about 2 minutes. Stir in tomatoes. Makes 6 servings.

Make tangy green tomato pickles with the last of the garden's tomatoes...it's so easy! Quarter the tomatoes and drop them into a jar of leftover dill pickle juice. Return the jar to the icebox for a few days before enjoying.

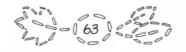

Cow-Country Beans

Debra Crisp
Merlin, OR

My family especially likes this recipe served over potato pancakes.

3 c. dried red beans
1 lb. cooked ham, cubed
1 onion, sliced
1 c. celery, diced
8-oz. can tomato sauce
2 T. bacon bits

2 T. chili powder
1 T. brown sugar, packed
2 t. garlic powder
1/2 t. smoke-flavored cooking
 sauce
1/2 t. salt

Cover dried beans with water in a bowl; soak overnight. In the morning, drain beans. Combine with remaining ingredients in a slow cooker. Cover and cook on high setting for 8 to 10 hours. Makes 8 to 10 servings.

No more boring drawer knobs! Glue on retro-style metal bottle caps...they're easy to find at flea markets and craft stores.

Garden-Fresh Salads & Sides

Amish Macaroni Salad

Diana Strawbridge
Ashtabula, OH

This macaroni salad is the best we've ever had! My aunt gave me the recipe...she lived near an Amish community in Ohio for many years and her Amish neighbor shared this with her.

8-oz. pkg. elbow macaroni,
    uncooked and divided
4 eggs, hard-boiled, peeled and
    chopped
1 onion, chopped
3 stalks celery, chopped
1 red pepper, chopped
1-1/2 c. mayonnaise-type salad
    dressing

3 T. mustard
2 T. dill pickle relish
1/2 c. sugar
2-1/4 t. white vinegar
3/4 t. celery seed
1/4 t. salt

Measure out 2 cups macaroni, reserving the rest for another recipe. Bring a pot of salted water to a boil. Add macaroni to pot and cook for 8 to 10 minutes, until tender. Drain and rinse with cool water. In a large bowl, stir together eggs and vegetables. In a small bowl, stir together remaining ingredients and pour over egg mixture. Stir in macaroni until well blended. Cover and chill for 2 hours to overnight before serving. Serves 8.

For a whimsical recipe card holder, hot-glue a clip clothespin to the handle of a tag-sale potato masher.

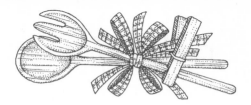

Creamy Bacon & Herb Succotash

Vickie

You'll love this deluxe version of an old harvest-time favorite...I do!

1/4 lb. bacon, chopped
1 onion, diced
10-oz. pkg. frozen lima beans
1/2 c. water
salt and pepper to taste

10-oz. pkg. frozen corn
1/2 c. whipping cream
1-1/2 t. fresh thyme, minced
Garnish: 2 t. fresh chives,
    snipped

In a Dutch oven over medium-high heat, cook bacon until crisp. Remove bacon, reserving 2 tablespoons drippings in Dutch oven. Add onion; sauté until tender, about 5 minutes. Add beans, water, salt and pepper; bring to a boil. Reduce heat; cover and simmer for 5 minutes. Stir in corn, cream and thyme; return to a simmer. Cook until vegetables are tender, about 5 minutes. Toss with reserved bacon and chives before serving. Makes 6 servings.

*A wheelbarrow makes a convenient planter for potted herbs...
it's so easy to wheel to the kitchen door and
snip off sprigs for cooking.*

Garden-Fresh Salads & Sides

Grandpa Jim's Potatoes

JoAnn Houghtby
Farmington, MN

After my grandma passed away, my grandpa learned to make coffee and cook for himself. It was just so adorable to see this 80-year-old man learning these skills for himself. This is a recipe that he was especially proud of...and it is SO good! He made it for our church potluck and it was a hit. I was so happy to go with him and see the twinkle in his eye.

8 to 10 potatoes, peeled, cooked and mashed

12-oz. pkg. bacon, crisply cooked and crumbled

8-oz. pkg. shredded Cheddar cheese

1-1/4 c. ranch salad dressing

Mix all ingredients together and spoon into a lightly greased 13"x9" baking pan. Bake, uncovered, at 375 degrees for 30 minutes, until heated through. Makes 12 to 15 servings.

A discarded window frame makes a memorable picture frame. Simply polish the panes with glass cleaner and place favorite photographs behind the openings. So sweet!

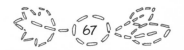

Good-for-You Southern Greens

Aubrey Dunne
Piscataway, NJ

On a wonderful trip down to North Carolina, our friends took us for authentic eastern North Carolina barbecue. We had some of the most delicious food we'd ever eaten. My husband loved the southern collard greens, but not all the fat they were cooked with. This recipe is my effort to make them a bit more healthy, but still serve up that down-home country flavor.

1/2 c. cooked ham, finely
   chopped
1/2 c. onion, finely chopped
1 bunch kale, trimmed

1/2 c. chicken broth
1/8 t. salt
1/8 t. pepper
Garnish: red wine vinegar

In a large skillet over medium heat, cook ham until slightly browned. Add remaining ingredients except vinegar. Cover; simmer for 15 minutes, or until kale turns soft and dark. Drizzle with vinegar to taste. Serves 4 to 6.

Sew up a quick shopping tote with snips of vintage fabrics like barkcloth and farmhouse calicos. It'll be so handy for carrying home goodies from the farmers' market!

Garden-Fresh Salads & Sides

Sweet-and-Sour Turnips

Barbara Ferree
New Freedom, PA

This Pennsylvania Dutch dish has been around for generations. We serve a community dinner at our church every year and I am always asked to bring my Sweet-and-Sour Turnips. I like them served with mashed potatoes.

5 to 6 turnips, peeled and sliced
    1/4-inch thick
salt to taste
1 egg, beaten

1/2 c. vinegar
1 c. sugar
1 T. all-purpose flour

Cover turnips with water in a large kettle; add salt as desired. Boil over medium-high heat until soft. Drain turnips thoroughly and return to kettle. Mix together egg, vinegar, sugar and flour until well blended. Add mixture to turnips and bring to a boil, stirring continuously to prevent scorching. Boil for approximately one minute; mixture will thicken slightly. Serves 4 to 6.

Create the perfect farmhouse porch with auction or tag-sale finds. Nothing says "country" like a porch swing and whitewashed wicker chairs...toss on pillows covered with vintage-print feedsacks.

Chopped Salad

JoEllen Ferington
Fountain Hills, AZ

*Serve alongside grilled sirloin or hamburgers and fresh-picked
ears of sweet corn...scrumptious!*

2 tomatoes, coarsely chopped
1/3 c. mayonnaise
1/2 t. salt
pepper to taste

1/4 t. cayenne pepper
1 head iceberg lettuce, chopped
6 thick slices bacon, crisply
   cooked and crumbled

Place tomatoes in a salad serving bowl; toss with mayonnaise and
seasonings. Cover and chill for 30 minutes to several hours. At
serving time, add lettuce and bacon to bowl. Stir to coat evenly.
Serves 4.

*For a fresh change from spinach, give Swiss chard a try.
An old-timey favorite that probably grew in your
grandmother's garden, it's easy to serve too...just steam
until tender, then drizzle with cider vinegar to taste.*

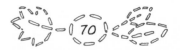

Garden-Fresh Salads & Sides

Cabbage Tomato Slaw

Tamara Parlor
Jacksonville, NC

This simple slaw tastes even better the next day!

1 head cabbage, chopped
1 sweet onion, chopped
2 tomatoes, diced

1/2 c. mayonnaise
salt and pepper to taste

Combine all ingredients in a large salad bowl. Toss to mix; cover and chill until serving time. Makes 6 servings.

There are always lots of yummy sides on the farmhouse table.
If you have a small family, or if there's just the two of you at
home, pick up a vintage divided serving dish or two...
they're just right for serving up lots of sides
without crowding the table.

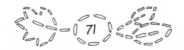

Creamy Cabbage Bake

Kimberly Burditt
Summerville, SC

This recipe is a favorite at our family cookouts...real comfort food.

1 head cabbage, coarsely
  chopped
1 c. carrots, peeled and chopped
1 c. onion, chopped
10-3/4 oz. can cream of
  mushroom soup
1/2 c. plus 2 T. milk

1/2 t. seasoned salt
1 t. dried parsley
8-oz. pkg. shredded Swiss
  cheese
8-oz. pkg. shredded Parmesan
  cheese

Boil cabbage, carrots and onion in water till tender; drain. Combine with remaining ingredients. Put into a greased 13"x9" baking pan. Bake, uncovered, at 350 degrees for 45 minutes. Serves 12.

Seasoned Summer Squash

Debbie Jurczyk
Gilbertville, MA

So simple and so delicious! Our family never tires of this recipe when summer squash is in season.

1 cube beef bouillon
4 to 6 yellow squash, sliced
  1/4-inch thick

1 onion, sliced 1/4-inch thick
Garnish: butter, seasoned salt,
  pepper

Place bouillon cube and one inch water in a medium saucepan. Layer squash and onion slices in pan. Cover; bring to a boil over medium-high heat. Reduce to medium heat; boil gently until tender, 5 to 8 minutes. Drain well. Serve in individual bowls as a side, allowing each person to add butter, salt and pepper to taste. Serves 6.

Whip up a quick & easy valance for a kitchen window...
just drape several flowered tea towels over the curtain rod.

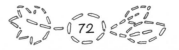

Scalloped Zucchini

Liz Gatewood
Madison, IN

We own a farm and raise veggies so we always have plenty of zucchini. I have come up with different ways to cook it and my family loves this recipe. Choose small and medium zucchini...they're more tender than the really big ones.

4 to 5 zucchini, sliced
1 onion, sliced
2 c. pasteurized process cheese
   spread, sliced

1 sleeve rectangular buttery
   crackers, crushed
1/2 c. butter, sliced

Layer half each of zucchini, onion and cheese slices in a buttered 13"x9" baking pan. Repeat layering. Top with crackers and dot with butter. Bake, uncovered, at 325 degrees until tender, about 40 minutes. Serves 8 to 10.

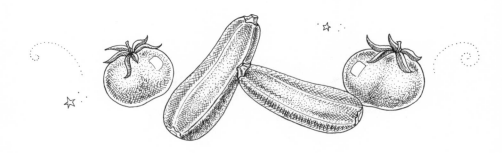

Look for heirloom fruits & vegetables at farmers' markets... varieties that Grandma & Grandpa may have grown in their garden. These fruits and veggies don't always look picture-perfect but their flavor can't be beat.

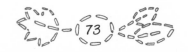

Mixed-Up Pasta Salad

Kathy Doty
Dover, DE

A great recipe for large get-togethers...everyone loves this! You can use any combination of pasta shells, wheels, twists and tubes.

12-oz. pkg. tri-color mixed
    pasta shapes, uncooked
14-1/2 oz. can green beans,
    drained
14-1/2 oz. can wax beans,
    drained
14-1/2 oz. can kidney beans,
    drained and rinsed

1 c. sweet onion, chopped
1/2 c. olive oil
3/4 c. cider vinegar
2/3 c. sugar
Optional: 1/2 c. cherry tomatoes,
    halved
salt and pepper to taste

Cook pasta according to package directions; drain and rinse with cold water. Meanwhile, combine beans and onion in a large bowl; set aside. In a separate bowl, combine oil and vinegar; slowly add sugar and stir until dissolved. Add pasta, tomatoes and oil mixture to bean mixture. Sprinkle with salt and pepper. Toss gently; serve immediately or refrigerate until serving time. Serves 10 to 12.

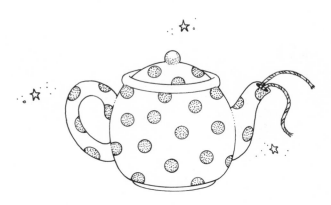

Keep a ball of kitchen string right where you need it!
Simply drop it into a small teapot and pull out the
end of the string through the spout.

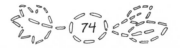

Garden-Fresh Salads & Sides

Red Pickled Eggs & Beets

Jane Brediger
Massillon, OH

*This recipe was my mother's. It is now on the third generation.
My 4-year-old grandson calls them "pink eggs" and just
loves them! I make them in a half-gallon ice tea jar.*

8 eggs, hard-boiled and peeled
1 sweet onion, thinly sliced
2 15-oz. cans small red beets,
   drained and juice reserved

1-1/2 c. cider vinegar
1-1/2 c. sugar

Place eggs in a large glass jar. Top with onion and beets; set aside.
Measure reserved beet juice and pour into a saucepan. Add equal
parts of vinegar and sugar (for example: to one cup beet juice, add
cup sugar and one cup vinegar). Bring just to a boil; stir to dissolve
sugar. Let cool for 5 minutes. Pour over eggs and beets, filling jar to
top. Cover; refrigerate for at least 2 days before serving. Makes
8 servings.

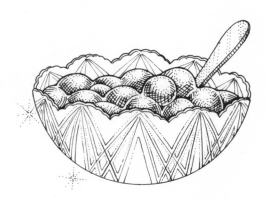

*An antique cut-glass serving dish really shows off the sparkling
color of ruby red beets, bright green bread & butter pickles,
sunny apricot jam and other homemade preserves.*

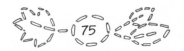

Bacon & Onion Mashed Potatoes

Sue Waldman
Chicago, IL

Gram and Mom used to fix mashed potatoes this delicious way...
I thought everybody did! Then I found out they did not, so why
not share. This is a good side dish with smoked meat or pork chops.

4 potatoes, peeled and quartered   2 c. green onions, green tops
3 slices bacon, chopped   only, sliced

Cover potatoes with water in a medium saucepan; boil until tender.
When potatoes are cooked, drain, leaving potatoes in pan. Place pan
back over low heat, shaking slightly to allow potatoes to dry. Remove
from heat again; mash potatoes and set aside. Fry bacon in a skillet
until crisp. Turn heat down to low; do not drain. Add onions, stirring
to coat all. Add potatoes, mashing to blend in bacon, drippings and
onions. Makes 4 servings.

Frame cherished handwritten recipes to hang in the kitchen.
They'll bring back sweet memories and will always
be nearby when you want to prepare them.

Cornbread Sage Dressing

Rosanna Dyck
Lime Springs, IA

This dressing comes from the heart of Dixie, where we used to live in Georgia and where we learned to love southern foods. Now that we live in Iowa, it is still our favorite with roast turkey.

13"x9" baking pan cornbread, crumbled
9 slices day-old white bread, torn

5 c. chicken broth or milk
1 T. dried sage
1/2 T. salt

Combine all ingredients in a very large bowl; toss together lightly. Spoon into a slow cooker. Cover and cook on low setting for about 3 hours. Makes 12 to 15 servings.

Homemade Cornbread:

3 eggs, beaten
1/2 c. water
1/2 c. margarine, melted
1 c. milk

1/2 c. onion, chopped
3/4 c. celery, chopped
1-1/2 c. self-rising cornmeal

Beat eggs and water; add remaining ingredients and mix well. Pour batter into a greased 13"x9" baking pan. Bake at 400 degrees for 30 minutes, until set and golden. Let cool.

A farmhouse kitchen favorite...knitted cotton dishcloths are a quick & easy project, even for beginning knitters. Why not give it a try?

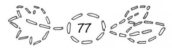

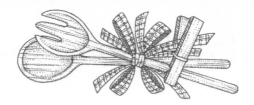

Cheesy Spinach Baked Ziti

Lori Ritchey
Denver, PA

When I serve this tasty dish, everyone is happy to eat their spinach!

12-oz. pkg. ziti pasta, cooked
14-1/2 oz. can diced tomatoes
   with Italian herbs
9-oz. pkg. frozen creamed
   spinach, thawed

8-oz. pkg. grated Romano
   cheese
8-oz. pkg. shredded mozzarella
   cheese

Mix all ingredients except mozzarella cheese; spread in a greased 13"x9" baking pan. Top with mozzarella cheese. Cover and bake at 350 degrees for 30 minutes, until hot and bubbly. Serves 4.

Add a little sugar when boiling corn on the cob or simmering homemade tomato sauce. It brings out the natural sweetness and reduces any bitterness. Just a pinch will do!

Gnocchi & Vegetable Toss

Jennifer Patrick
Delaware, OH

This mixture of tender little potato dumplings and colorful veggies is almost a meal in itself.

17-1/2 oz. pkg. potato gnocchi, uncooked
1 lb. asparagus, cut into bite-size pieces
1 zucchini, halved and sliced
1 yellow squash, halved and sliced

10-oz. pkg. grape tomatoes, halved
10-oz. jar sun-dried tomato-basil pesto sauce
1/2 c. sour cream

In a stockpot, bring 4 quarts of water to a boil. Add gnocchi and vegetables. Return to a boil; boil for 2 to 3 minutes, until gnocchi floats to top; drain. Mix pesto sauce with sour cream. Add to gnocchi mixture; toss until coated thoroughly. Serve hot or cold. Makes 4 to 6 servings.

Snap up oversized letters at flea markets to spell out whimsical words...like EAT on a dining room wall or GROW on a garden fence!

German Hot Potato Salad

Jennifer Savino
Joliet, IL

My grandma was famous for this recipe...she'd bring a huge bowl
to share at every family or community occasion.
Definitely a comfort food and so delicious!

6 slices bacon, finely chopped
1 onion, sliced
1/3 c. vinegar
1/2 c. water
2 t. all-purpose flour
1 T. sugar

1-1/2 t. salt
1/4 t. pepper
1/2 c. fresh parsley, chopped
1-1/4 lbs. potatoes, peeled,
    sliced and cooked

In a large skillet, sauté bacon until crisp. Drain off most of drippings;
add onion and sauté for 2 minutes. Add remaining ingredients except
potatoes; cook and stir until thickened. Add potatoes and stir well.
Serve warm. Makes 4 to 6 servings.

Vintage days-of-the-week towels make such sweet
window toppers...just attach clip-on curtain rings.

Green Bean Bundles

Wendy Sensing
Brentwood, TN

Easy and delicious! This is one of our favorite side dishes to bring to church get-togethers. The dish always comes home empty and someone always wants the recipe, especially the garlic lovers.

3 14-1/2 oz. cans whole green
  beans, drained
8 slices bacon, cut in half
  crosswise

6 T. butter, melted
1/2 c. brown sugar, packed
2 to 3 cloves garlic, minced

Gather beans in bundles of 10; wrap each bundle with a half-slice of bacon. Arrange bundles in a lightly greased 13"x9" baking pan. Mix melted butter, sugar and garlic in small bowl; spoon over bundles. Cover and bake at 375 degrees for 30 minutes. Uncover; bake an additional 15 minutes. Serves 6.

*Turn leftover mashed potatoes into twice-baked potatoes.
Stir in minced onion, crumbled bacon and shredded cheese
to taste and pat into individual ramekins. Bake at
350 degrees until hot and golden...delicious!*

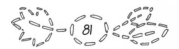

Broccoli-Cauliflower Salad

Janice Tarter
Morrow, OH

We grow our own vegetables on our country farm, so I'm always looking for new ways to serve fresh veggies. This is a very refreshing salad...great to make ahead and take to a picnic. It's very easy and very yummy!

1 head broccoli, chopped
1 head cauliflower, chopped
1 c. green onions, chopped
1/2 lb. bacon, crisply cooked
   and crumbled

1 c. mayonnaise-type salad
   dressing
1/2 c. sugar

Combine broccoli, cauliflower, onions and bacon in a large salad bowl. Mix dressing and sugar in a separate bowl. Drizzle over broccoli mixture; toss all together. Serve immediately or refrigerate until serving time. Serves 6 to 8.

A well-used wooden salad bowl is a terrific thrift-shop find. To restore the bowl's glowing finish, sand lightly inside and out with fine sandpaper. Rub a little vegetable oil over the bowl and let stand overnight, then wipe off any excess oil in the morning. It will be good as new!

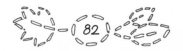

Garden-Fresh Salads & Sides

Teresa's Easy-Peasy Salad

Teresa Ponder
Deland, FL

This salad was always served at holiday dinners year 'round when I was growing up...everyone liked the crunchy textures and the slightly sweet dressing. Now I make it for the holidays for my own family and for potlucks at work or church.

1 head lettuce, shredded
3 to 4 stalks celery, chopped
16-oz. pkg. frozen peas, cooked
   and cooled

1 lb. bacon, crisply cooked and
   crumbled

Place lettuce in a large salad bowl; layer with celery, peas and bacon. Serve with Special Dressing on the side, or pour dressing over salad at serving time. Keep refrigerated. Serves 6 to 8.

Special Dressing:

1-1/2 c. mayonnaise-type salad
   dressing
1/4 c. sugar

1 to 2 T. milk, divided

Mix together salad dressing and sugar. Add milk, one tablespoon at a time, until desired consistency is reached.

A whimsical kitchen decoration... vintage fruit crate labels from the 1930's and 1940's were always decorated with such fun designs. Look for them at flea markets or barn sales.

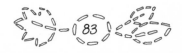

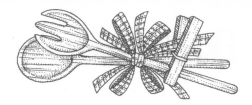

Mary's Baked Macaroni

Paula Weaver
Steeleville, IL

My mother's recipe for special dinners and company.

8-oz. pkg. elbow macaroni,
  uncooked and divided
1-1/2 c. milk
2 T. cornstarch
1/3 c. water
1-1/2 c. Colby Longhorn cheese,
  diced

3 eggs, beaten
1/2 c. oil
1 onion, diced
1/2 green pepper, diced
8-oz. can sliced mushrooms,
  drained
1 to 2 c. soda crackers, crushed

Measure out 1-1/2 cups macaroni, reserving the rest for another
recipe. Cook macaroni according to package directions; drain. Heat
milk, without bringing to a boil, in a saucepan over medium heat.
In a small bowl, whisk together cornstarch and water; slowly stir into
warmed milk. Cook just until slightly thickened, about 2 minutes.
Combine macaroni and milk mixture with remaining ingredients
except cracker crumbs. Pour into a buttered 3-quart casserole dish.
Cover with cracker crumbs. Bake, covered, at 350 degrees for one
hour, until golden. Serves 6 to 8.

*Tuck packets of gravy and seasoning mix into a
napkin holder to keep the pantry tidy.*

Farmhouse Egg Noodles

Angela Miller
Jefferson City, MO

*These scrumptious homemade noodles have been a tradition in
our family for many years. Unrolling the noodles has always
been the children's job...they love helping out!*

1 c. all-purpose flour	1/8 t. salt
1 egg, beaten	3 to 4 14-1/2 oz. cans chicken
3 T. milk	broth

Place flour in a large bowl; make a well in the center and add egg,
milk and salt. Slowly stir to mix in flour until a soft ball forms; knead
in any remaining flour. Roll out dough on a floured surface to about
1/4-inch thick. Roll up dough jelly-roll style; slice across to cut
noodles about 1/2-inch wide. Unroll noodles and pile them on a
floured surface while waiting for broth to warm. In a large saucepan,
bring broth to a boil. Drop noodles into broth. Cook until tender, about
8 to 10 minutes. Makes 4 to 6 servings.

*Homemade chicken broth is simple to make. Whenever you
simmer chicken for a recipe, save the liquid and freeze it. When
it's time to make broth, thaw and combine with the desired
amount of chopped onion, chopped carrots and sliced celery.
Simmer, uncovered, for one hour and strain.*

Tomato-Basil Pasta Bake

Lori Van Antwerp
Gooseberry Patch

Your family will love the fresh taste of the homemade pasta sauce...
it's simple to make using canned tomatoes.

2/3 c. onion, chopped
2 cloves garlic, minced
2 T. butter
28-oz. can diced tomatoes with
   Italian herbs
2 T. fresh basil, snipped
1/2 t. sugar

1/4 t. pepper
Optional: 1 T. capers, drained
8-oz. pkg. thin spaghetti,
   uncooked and divided
1/2 c. shredded mozzarella
   cheese

In a large skillet, sauté onion and garlic in butter until onion is tender. Stir in tomatoes with juice and seasonings. Bring to a boil; reduce heat. Simmer, uncovered, for about 20 minutes. Stir in capers, if using; remove from heat. Meanwhile, measure out half the spaghetti, reserving the rest for another recipe. Cook according to package directions. Drain spaghetti and add to skillet; toss to coat with sauce. Spoon into a lightly greased 9"x9" baking pan. Sprinkle with cheese. Bake at 400 degrees for 5 to 8 minutes, or until bubbly and cheese is melted. Serves 4.

Treat yourself to a bar or two of handmade herbal soap and savor the scent everyday, not just in the bath! Keep a fragrant bar of lemon verbena soap at the kitchen sink for quick wash-ups or tuck an unwrapped bar of lavender soap into a drawer of tea towels. Ahhh!

Spanish Hominy

Megan Brooks
Antioch, TN

Use either white or yellow hominy for this old-fashioned side.

2 29-oz. cans hominy, drained
14-1/2 oz. can diced tomatoes
10-oz. can diced tomatoes with
   chiles

8-oz. can tomato sauce
3/4 lb. bacon, diced
1 onion, chopped
1 green pepper, chopped

Combine hominy, both cans of tomatoes in juice and tomato sauce in a slow cooker; set aside. In a skillet over medium heat, cook bacon until crisp. Remove bacon to a paper towel-covered plate. Drain skillet, reserving one tablespoon drippings. Add onion and pepper; sauté until tender. Stir onion mixture and bacon into mixture in slow cooker. Cover and cook on low setting for 6 to 8 hours. Makes 8 to 10 servings.

Try your hand at vegetable gardening! Even the smallest yard is sure to have a sunny corner where you can grow sun-ripened tomatoes and an herb plant or two. Or, fill a wooden half-barrel with potting soil and plant a mini garden. Seeds, plants and free advice are available at the nearest garden store.

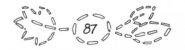

Tyler's Strawberry Tapioca

Maureen Froemming
Darwin, MN

*I make this salad quite often when we get together for family
birthday parties. It is my nephew Tyler's favorite salad.
This is a great make-ahead recipe.*

5 c. water
3/4 t. salt
1/2 c. plus 1 T. pearl tapioca,
   uncooked
1 c. sugar
3-oz. pkg. strawberry gelatin
   mix

8-oz. container frozen whipped
   topping, thawed
2 c. strawberries, hulled and
   sliced

In a large saucepan, combine water and salt. Bring to a boil over
medium heat. Add tapioca; cook for 20 minutes. Remove from heat;
stir in sugar and gelatin mix. Pour into a large serving bowl; cover
and refrigerate overnight. At serving time, stir gelatin to break up; fold
in whipped topping and berries. Makes 12 servings.

At country potlucks and carry-ins,
fruity gelatin salads are yummy
when topped with a dollop of
creamy lemon mayonnaise.
Stir 3 tablespoons each of
lemon juice, light cream and
powdered sugar into 1/2 cup
mayonnaise. Garnish with a
sprinkle of lemon zest, if you like.

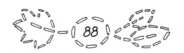

Raspberry Pretzel Salad

Gean Wilson
Greenwater, WA

*A neighbor shared this recipe with me during a neighborhood barbecue.
Now I take this along to any barbecues I attend. The next day,
people always call me to ask for the recipe.*

1-1/2 c. pretzels, crushed
1/2 c. sugar
1/2 c. butter, melted
8-oz. pkg. cream cheese,
  softened
1/2 c. sugar

8-oz. container frozen whipped
  topping, thawed
6-oz. pkg. raspberry gelatin mix
2 c. boiling water
2 10-oz. pkgs. frozen
  raspberries

Mix pretzels, sugar and butter; press into the bottom of an ungreased
13"x9" baking pan to form a crust. Bake at 350 degrees for 5 to
7 minutes; let cool. Combine cream cheese, sugar and whipped
topping; spread over baked crust and chill. Combine gelatin mix and
boiling water in a medium bowl; chill until partially set. Stir in frozen
berries; spread over cream cheese layer. Refrigerate until serving time.
Makes 12 to 15 servings.

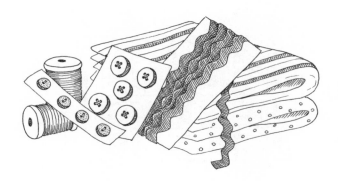

*Thrifty farm wives always used cotton kitchen towels...they're
still a great alternative to toss-away paper towels. Dress up
plain-Jane towels by stitching on narrow bands of vintage
quilting fabric and a row or two of rick rack.*

Tried & True Apple Casserole

Gerry Donnella
Boston, VA

Whenever I would fry apples they turned out like applesauce, until a friend said, "I have a recipe you will love." She was right...I've been using it ever since and it NEVER fails! This is a great potluck dish.

8 to 10 tart apples, cored, peeled
    and halved
1/2 c. sugar
1/2 t. cinnamon

1/4 t. nutmeg
1 T. all-purpose flour
2 T. butter

Place apples in a buttered 2-quart casserole dish; set aside. Mix dry ingredients together; sprinkle over apples. Dot with butter. Cover and bake at 350 degrees for 45 minutes to one hour. Serves 6 to 8.

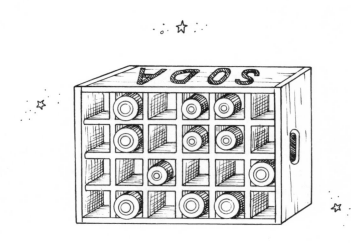

A vintage wooden soda crate makes a handy spice rack...hang it on the wall or simply stand it up on the kitchen counter.

Cozy Soups & Breads

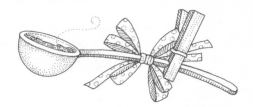

Mushroom-Barley Soup

Holly Vidourek
Cincinnati, OH

Rich and hearty...always a family favorite.

1/2 lb. stew beef, cubed
1 onion, chopped
8-oz. pkg. sliced mushrooms

1 T. olive oil
4 14-1/2 oz. cans beef broth
3/4 c. instant barley, uncooked

Combine beef, onion, mushrooms and oil in a large saucepan. Cook over medium-high heat for about 10 minutes, until beef is browned. Stir in broth; bring to a boil. Add barley. Reduce heat and simmer, covered, for 30 to 45 minutes, until beef and barley are tender. Serves 4 to 6.

Yellowware soup bowls make any soup supper extra special.
Pick up a set of vintage-style new bowls or collect old ones at
antique shops...mix & match for fresh farmhouse style.

Cozy Soups & Breads

Potato Patch Soup

Corrie Leydig
Hyndman, PA

*This recipe is my mother's...every couple of weeks, she was sure
to have this soup waiting for us on the stove.*

7 potatoes, peeled and diced
1 carrot, peeled and finely
   chopped
2 T. dried, minced onion
3 c. water
4 cubes chicken bouillon

1 T. dried parsley
1 t. celery seed
4 slices pasteurized process
   cheese spread
1-1/2 c. milk

Combine potatoes, carrot, onion, water, bouillon cubes, parsley and
celery seed in a large saucepan. Simmer over medium heat until
potatoes are tender, 25 to 30 minutes. Remove from heat. Add cheese
slices; let stand until melted. Stir in milk and serve. Serves 5 to 7.

No matter where I serve my guests,
They seem to like my kitchen best.
-Old Saying

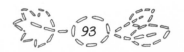

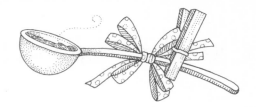

Cheese-Stuffed Biscuits

Angie Venable
Gooseberry Patch

My kind of recipe...down-home goodness, ready to serve in a jiffy!

10-oz. tube refrigerated flaky
  biscuits
8-oz. pkg. Cheddar cheese,
  sliced into 10 cubes

1 T. milk
1 t. poppy seed

Separate dough into 10 biscuits. Open a small pocket in the side of each biscuit; tuck a cheese cube into each pocket. Press dough together to seal well. Place biscuits on an ungreased baking sheet. Cut a deep "X" in the top of each biscuit. Brush with milk and sprinkle with poppy seed. Bake at 400 degrees for 10 to 12 minutes, until golden. Serve warm. Makes 10.

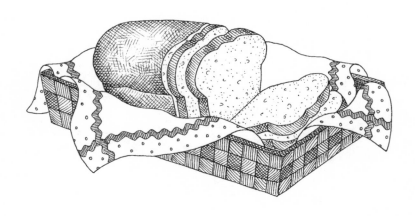

Slip a prewarmed ceramic tile into the bread basket before adding a napkin liner. Biscuits and rolls will stay toasty and warm through dinner.

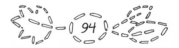

Cozy Soups & Breads

Tomato & Basil Bisque

Zoe Bennett
Columbia, SC

Garnish servings with a swirl of cream and a sprig of basil leaves.

2 onions, chopped
2 carrots, peeled and shredded
1 T. butter
8 tomatoes, peeled and chopped
1/2 t. sugar

1/2 t. salt
1/4 t. pepper
1/2 c. fresh basil, chopped
2 c. chicken broth

In a large saucepan over medium heat, sauté onions and carrots in butter until tender. Stir in tomatoes, sugar, salt and pepper; bring to a boil. Reduce heat; cover and simmer for 10 minutes. Cool soup slightly; transfer to a blender. Add basil; cover and process until smooth. Pour soup back into saucepan. Stir in broth; heat through. Serves 4.

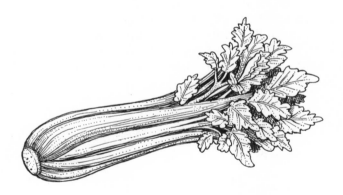

Dried celery leaves add homestyle flavor to soups and stews. Save the leaves from celery stalks, spread them on a baking sheet and dry slowly in a 180-degree oven for 3 hours. When they're crisp and dry, store them in a canning jar. The leaves can be crumbled right into a simmering soup pot.

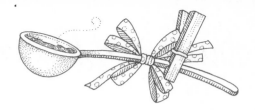

Teri's Butternut Squash Soup

Teri Johnson
North Ogden, UT

*We tried a delicious squash soup at a local restaurant. This recipe
is my own version and it's so good! We find it's also good
served chilled, with sliced green onions on top.*

1 T. olive oil
1 T. butter
2 2-lb. butternut squash, peeled
   and cubed
1 onion, chopped

1 clove garlic, minced
1/2 t. allspice
2 14-1/2 oz. cans chicken broth
Garnish: sour cream, saltine
   crackers

Combine oil and butter in a large saucepan over medium heat.
Add squash, onion and garlic. Cook for about 5 minutes, stirring
occasionally, until crisp-tender. Add allspice; cook just a minute more.
Add broth. Bring to a boil; cover. Reduce heat to low; simmer for
15 minutes, or until squash is tender. Mash with a potato masher
or use an immersion stick blender to blend until smooth. Return to
saucepan; heat until hot. If a thinner soup is preferred, add a little
more broth or water. Ladle soup into 8 soup bowls. Add one
tablespoon sour cream to each bowl and swirl slightly. Serve with
crackers. Serves 8.

*A pretty cut-glass biscuit jar
isn't just for holding cookies
or crackers...fill it with crisp
bread sticks or pretzel rods
to serve with soup.*

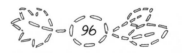

Cozy Soups & Breads

Cream of Zucchini Soup

Susan Maurer
Dahlgren, IL

*One taste and you'll agree...there's really no such thing
as too many zucchini!*

3 lbs. zucchini, sliced 1/2-inch
   thick
2 onions, quartered
5 slices bacon
4 c. chicken broth
1 t. salt

1 t. pepper
Optional: 1/2 t. garlic powder
Garnish: onion and garlic
   croutons or butter and
   grated Parmesan cheese

Combine all ingredients except garnish in a soup pot over medium heat. Cook until zucchini is tender and bacon is done, about 45 minutes. Ladle soup into a blender and process until smooth. Return to soup pot; heat through. Serve topped with croutons or with a pat of butter and a sprinkling of Parmesan cheese. Makes 4 to 6 servings.

*Save time when peeling and chopping veggies. Set a large
bowl on the counter to toss all the peelings into...
you'll only need to empty it once.*

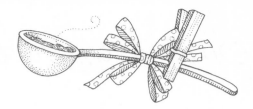

Monk's Bean Soup

*Staci Meyers
Montezuma, GA*

*My cousin Monk came to visit once and brought us a pot of this
yummy soup. I wouldn't let him leave until he shared the recipe!*

1 to 2 smoked ham hocks
6 to 8 c. water
2 T. butter
1 onion, chopped
3 to 5 T. dill weed

seasoned salt and pepper to
taste
16-oz. pkg. dried Great
Northern beans

Combine ham hocks and water in a large soup pot. Simmer over
medium heat for 15 to 30 minutes. Melt butter in a skillet; add onion
and seasonings. Cook for about 5 minutes, just until onion is tender.
Place beans in a slow cooker; add onion mixture, then pour meat and
broth over top. Cover and cook on high setting for 4 to 6 hours, until
beans are as tender as desired. Shortly before serving time, dice meat
from ham hocks and stir back into slow cooker. Makes 8 servings.

*Pile seasonal produce in a primitive wooden dough bowl for a
bountiful country-style centerpiece...shiny red and yellow
peppers in summer, acorn squash and gourds in autumn.*

Tadpole Ham Soup

Sara Goodroe
Moultrie, GA

A family recipe we've used for generations...the small onion pieces gave this wonderful southern dish its funny name.

2 c. cooked ham, cubed
1 c. pan drippings from a baked
   ham
4 to 5 green onions, cut into
   one-inch pieces

4 c. water
pepper to taste

Put ham cubes, pan drippings, onions and water into a soup pot. Bring to a slow boil over medium heat; simmer for 10 minutes. While soup is boiling, drop dumplings by tablespoonfuls into the pot. Slowly cook until dumplings are done, about 20 minutes. Add a little more water if soup seems too thick. Add pepper to taste. Serves 4.

Dumplings:

1 egg, beaten

1 c. self-rising flour

Combine egg and flour, working them together by hand until dough forms.

Stitch several handmade napkins or tea towels end-to-end to make a one-of-a-kind table runner.

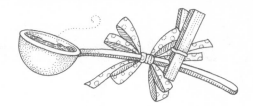

No-Knead Oatmeal Bread

Hattie Douthit
Crawford, NE

I've been making this bread since I was a little girl.
It's slightly sweet and so yummy.

2 envs. active dry yeast
1/2 c. warm water
1 c. quick-cooking oats,
  uncooked
1/2 c. light molasses
1/3 c. shortening

1-1/2 c. boiling water
1 T. salt
6-1/4 c. all-purpose flour,
  divided
2 eggs, beaten

Soften yeast in very warm water, 110 to 115 degrees; let stand for about 5 minutes. In a large bowl, combine oats, molasses, shortening, boiling water and salt; stir until shortening is melted. Cool until lukewarm. Stir in 2 cups of flour; add eggs and beat well. Stir in yeast mixture. Add remaining flour, 2 cups a time, mixing well after each addition to make a rather stiff dough. Beat vigorously until smooth, about 10 minutes. Grease top of dough lightly. Cover tightly; place in refrigerator for 2 hours to overnight. Turn dough out onto a well-floured surface. Form into 2 loaves; place in greased 8"x4" loaf pans. Cover; let rise in a warm place until double. Bake at 375 degrees for about 40 minutes. If crust begins to brown too fast, cover with aluminum foil for last half of baking time. Makes 2 loaves.

Here's how to tell when rising dough has doubled in size.
Press two fingertips into the dough, about 1/2-inch deep,
and then release. If the dent remains, the dough has doubled.

Honey Koek Loaf

Tawnia Hultink
Ontario, Canada

A nice easy-to-make Dutch bread...kids love it!

2 c. all-purpose flour
1 c. sugar
1 t. cinnamon
1/2 t. ground ginger
1/2 t. nutmeg
1/2 t. ground cloves

1 t. baking soda
1/2 t. baking powder
1/2 t. salt
1/2 c. honey
1 c. boiling water

Combine dry ingredients in a large bowl; mix all together. Add honey and boiling water; stir together. Pour batter into a greased 9"x5" loaf pan. Bake at 350 degrees for one hour. Cool in pan for 10 minutes; turn loaf out of the pan and cool on a wire rack. Makes one loaf.

Snap up stoneware butter crocks when you find them at flea markets. They're just the right size for serving party spreads and dips as well as butter.

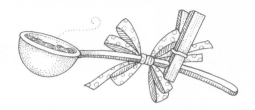

Country Comfort Chicken Soup

Rhonda Nehmer
Menomonee Falls, WI

Everyone needs a great recipe for chicken noodle soup! I love homemade soup but do not have enough time anymore to spend hours making it, so I created this simpler version.

5 to 6 boneless, skinless
   chicken thighs
2 c. baby carrots, chopped
1 c. celery, chopped
1/2 onion, chopped
2 T. garlic, minced

1 t. poultry seasoning
1 t. dried parsley
1 t. seasoned salt
3 cubes chicken bouillon
12-oz. pkg. fine egg noodles,
   uncooked

Place all ingredients except noodles into a large soup pot; cover with water. Bring to a boil; reduce heat to a simmer. Cook, uncovered, until chicken and vegetables are tender, about one hour. Remove chicken; let cool slightly. Stir in noodles. Simmer until noodles are done, about 5 minutes. While noodles are cooking, dice chicken and return to soup. Adjust seasoning as needed. Makes 8 servings.

Savory herbed crackers make any bowl of soup even yummier! Toss together 1-1/2 cups oyster crackers, 1-1/2 tablespoons melted butter, 1/4 teaspoon dried thyme and 1/4 teaspoon garlic powder. Spread on a baking sheet. Bake at 350 degrees for about 10 minutes, until crunchy and golden.

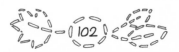

Cider Mill Stew

Laura Lett
Gooseberry Patch

This stew smells as wonderful as it tastes!

3 T. all-purpose flour
1 t. salt
1/2 t. pepper
1 lb. stew beef, cubed
2 T. oil
1 c. apple cider
1 c. water
1 c. beef broth

1 T. cider vinegar
1/2 t. dried thyme
2 carrots, peeled and cut into
  1-inch pieces
1 stalk celery, cut into 1-inch
  pieces
1 potato, peeled and cubed
1 onion, sliced

Combine flour, salt and pepper in a large plastic zipping bag. Add beef, a few pieces at a time; shake to coat. In a Dutch oven, brown beef in oil; drain. Stir in cider, water, broth vinegar and thyme; bring to a boil over medium heat. Reduce heat; cover and simmer for one hour and 45 minutes, or until meat is tender. Add vegetables; return to a boil. Reduce heat; cover and simmer for 30 minutes, or until vegetables are tender. Makes 4 servings.

Turn a mesh bag that held apples or onions into a sink scrubbie for cleaning veggies and washing dishes. Simply fold the bag several times into a loose bundle and wind with kitchen string. So thrifty...Grandma would be proud!

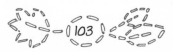

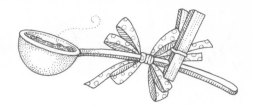

Squash & Sausage Stew

Debbie Gillam
Tipton, IN

My great-aunts Ardella and Clarissa were avid gardeners, so they had an abundance of fresh veggies. They devised this fresh and nutritious soup recipe that I've made often. It's even tastier as leftovers!

1 lb. smoked turkey sausage,
    cut in bite-size pieces
2 to 3 yellow squash, cut into
    1/2-inch cubes
2 to 3 zucchini, cut into
    1/2-inch cubes

2 14-1/2 oz. cans diced
    tomatoes
1 onion, chopped
2 to 3 cloves garlic, minced

Combine all ingredients in a large soup pot. Bring to a boil over medium-high heat. Reduce heat to low. Simmer until vegetables are tender, stirring occasionally, one to 2 hours. Serves 4 to 6.

Keep a few quart-size Mason jars tucked in the cupboard so you can send home some homemade soup with a dinner guest...what a thoughtful gesture!

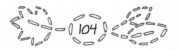

Cozy Soups & Breads

Down-Home Pea Soup

Jude Trimnal
Brevard, NC

*Our parents made this soup often. It is delicious year 'round,
but is especially warming on winter days.*

8 c. water
2 c. dried split peas
1-1/2 c. celery, sliced
1-1/2 c. carrots, peeled and
    sliced

1 onion, sliced
2 bay leaves
salt and pepper to taste
Optional: 1 to 2 c. cooked ham,
    cubed

Combine all ingredients in a slow cooker. Cover and cook on low
setting for 4 to 6 hours. Discard bay leaves before serving. Makes 8 to
10 servings.

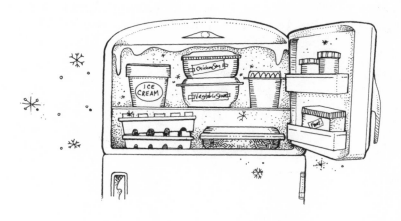

Don't pass up delicious-sounding recipes that make enough to
serve a farmhouse family when you only need to serve two.
Leftovers are great for next-day meals. Soups, stews and
casseroles make quick & easy lunches, or freeze leftovers
for a heat-and-serve meal later when time is short.

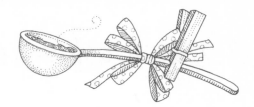

Old-Fashioned Icebox Rolls

Muriel Gundy
Morley, MI

A very old tried & true recipe from my mother and aunt.
This is also a good dough to use for making cinnamon rolls.

1 env. active dry yeast
1/4 c. warm water
1/2 c. boiling water
1/3 c. shortening
1/3 c. sugar

1/2 c. cold water
1/2 t. salt
1 egg, beaten
3-3/4 c. all-purpose flour

In a small bowl, combine yeast and very warm water, 110 to
115 degrees; let stand for several minutes. In a separate large bowl,
pour boiling water over shortening and sugar. Add yeast mixture, cold
water, salt, egg and flour. Mix and knead until smooth. Cover and
place in refrigerator overnight. Form into golfball-size balls and place
in a greased 13"x9" baking pan. Cover; let rise until double. Bake at
400 degrees for 12 to 18 minutes, until golden. Makes 2 dozen.

It's easy to turn a vintage painted metal tray into a whimsical
wall clock with a clock kit from your local craft store. Drill
a center hole, then insert the clock movement and hands.
Press on self-adhesive numbers...time's up!

Cozy Soups & Breads

North Woods Bean Soup

Sharon Demers
Dolores, CO

Here is a great soup to come home to on a brisk, cool evening.

1/2 lb. turkey Kielbasa, halved
   lengthwise and sliced
   1/2-inch thick
1 c. baby carrots, chopped
1 c. onion, chopped
2 cloves garlic, minced

4 c. chicken broth
1/2 t. Italian seasoning
1/2 t. pepper
2 15.8-oz. cans Great Northern
   beans, drained and rinsed
6-oz. pkg. baby spinach

Spray a large stockpot with non-stick vegetable spray; heat over medium-high heat. Add Kielbasa, carrots, onion and garlic; sauté for 3 minutes, stirring occasionally. Reduce heat to medium; cook for 5 minutes. Add broth, seasonings and beans. Bring to a boil; reduce heat and simmer for 5 minutes. Place 2 cups of soup in a blender or food processor. Process until smooth; return processed soup to pan. Simmer for an additional 5 minutes; remove from heat. Add spinach, stirring until it wilts. Serves 5.

Nothing goes better with hearty bean and pea soup than warm cornbread! If you like your cornbread crisp, prepare it in a vintage sectioned cast-iron skillet...each wedge of cornbread will bake up with its own golden crust.

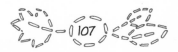

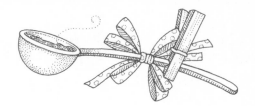

Farmhouse Onion Soup

Irene Whatling
West Des Moines, IA

With four kinds of onions and two kinds of cheese,
this savory soup is a meal in itself.

2 T. butter
1 yellow onion, thinly sliced
1 red onion, thinly sliced
1 leek, white part only, sliced
5 green onions, sliced
1 clove garlic, minced
2 14-1/2 oz. cans beef broth

10-1/2 oz. can beef consommé
1 t. Worcestershire sauce
1/2 t. ground nutmeg
1 c. shredded Swiss cheese,
   divided
6 slices French bread, toasted
6 T. grated Parmesan cheese

Melt butter in a large saucepan over medium-low heat. Sauté all
onions and garlic, stirring occasionally, until tender and golden, about
15 minutes. Add broth, consommé, Worcestershire sauce and nutmeg;
bring to a boil. Reduce heat; cover and simmer for 30 minutes.
Sprinkle one tablespoon Swiss cheese into each of 6 oven-proof soup
bowls. Ladle soup into bowls; top each with a slice of toasted bread.
Sprinkle bread with remaining Swiss and Parmesan. Broil until cheese
is melted; serve right away. Serves 6.

A pretty china saucer that has lost its teacup can still
be useful. Place it beside the stovetop to serve as
a rest for cooking spoons and soup ladles.

Kale & Potato Soup

Maureen Viggiani
North Chili, NY

A quick, healthy soup for a blustery day. Make it heartier by adding
1/2 pound ground turkey sausage that has been browned and drained.

1 T. oil
1 onion, chopped
1/2 bunch kale, chopped

1 to 2 redskin potatoes, cubed
4 c. chicken broth

Heat oil in a medium saucepan over medium heat. Add onion and
cook until translucent. Add kale, potato, broth and sausage, if using.
Cover and simmer 15 minutes, until potato is tender. Serves 4 to 6.

Use lemon juice to freshen an old wooden breadboard.
Brush juice generously over the surface and let stand
for 30 minutes. Then scrub with a moistened cloth
and a little baking soda, rinse and let dry.

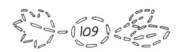

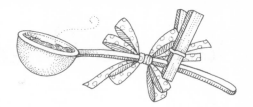

Champion Banana Bread

Michelle Mahler
Osceola, WI

My grandma taught me most of what I know about baking. This simple recipe was hers...I wish I knew where she got it! I even won the Champion Ribbon at the county fair with this recipe when I was a young girl. My family belongs to a little old country church and it has been published in their cookbook several times as well.

2 eggs, beaten
1/2 c. butter, softened
1 c. sugar
3 bananas, mashed
1/2 c. evaporated milk

1 t. vanilla extract
1 t. baking powder
1 t. baking soda
1/2 t. salt
2 c. all-purpose flour

Blend eggs, butter and sugar; add bananas, milk and vanilla. Stir in dry ingredients; mix well. Pour batter into a 9"x5" loaf pan that has been sprayed with non-stick vegetable spray. Bake at 350 degrees for 40 to 50 minutes. Makes one loaf.

Make a new neighbor feel welcome by giving a loaf of homemade bread, wrapped in a checked napkin and tucked into a wicker basket.

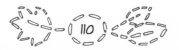

Mom's Raisin Bread

Suzanne Pletsch
Chicago, IL

*Everyone loved Mom's raisin bread. When I got married,
Mom gave me the recipe...I finally got her to actually
measure ingredients! My children love it too.*

1 c. milk
1/4 c. margarine
2 t. salt
1/2 c. golden raisins
1 env. active dry rapid-rise yeast
2 T. sugar

1/2 c. warm water
2 eggs, beaten
5 c. all-purpose flour, divided
Garnish: beaten egg, milk or
   softened margarine

In a small saucepan over low heat, heat milk just to boiling; stir in margarine and salt. Add raisins and let cool. In a large saucepan, combine yeast, sugar and very warm water, 110 to 115 degrees. When milk mixture cools, add it to yeast mixture; stir in eggs. Beat in flour, one cup at a time. When dough gets heavier, start to knead it, adding more flour if too sticky. Knead for about 10 minutes. Place dough in a large greased pan; cover. Set pan in an unheated oven with a pan of hot water placed below it. Let rise for one hour. Punch dough down; let rise for an additional 30 minutes. Knead dough again; form into 2 loaves and place in 2 greased 8-1/2"x4-1/2" loaf pans. Cover and let rise again for 30 minutes. Brush loaves with egg, milk or margarine. Bake at 375 degrees until golden, 45 to 60 minutes. Makes 2 loaves.

*Grandma's little secret...kneading bread dough is a fun way
to get rid of stress! Be sure to knead the dough as long
as the recipe states, until the dough is silky smooth.
You'll be rewarded with moist, tender bread.*

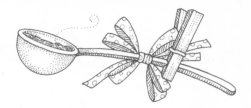

Chunky Minestrone

Sharon Ignash
Kinde, MI

This recipe has been a huge hit at soup luncheons, at family gatherings and at work. It's easy to make and low calorie for calorie watchers. We all just love it and hope you will too!

1 T. olive oil
1-1/2 c. onion, chopped
1 carrot, peeled and sliced
2 cloves garlic, minced
14-1/2 oz. can diced tomatoes
4 c. chicken broth
1 c. water
1 t. Italian seasoning

1/2 c. long-cooking rice or soup pasta, uncooked
15-oz. can kidney beans, drained and rinsed
1 zucchini, chopped
1/2 t. pepper
Garnish: grated Parmesan cheese

In a Dutch oven, heat oil over medium heat. Add onion, carrot and garlic; cook for 3 minutes, or until tender. Stir in tomatoes with juice, broth, water, seasoning and uncooked rice or pasta. Bring to a boil. Reduce heat and simmer, uncovered, for 20 minutes or until rice or pasta is tender. Stir in beans, zucchini and pepper; simmer for 5 minutes. Sprinkle with cheese before serving. Makes 5 servings.

Keep hard grating cheeses like Parmesan fresh for longer.
Wrap the cheese in a paper towel that has been
moistened with cider vinegar, tuck into a
plastic zipping bag and refrigerate.

Meatball Vegetable Soup

Sally Derkenne
Chandler, AZ

The made-from-scratch meatballs are really tasty,
but if time is short, substitute frozen meatballs.

4 c. beef broth
2-1/2 c. water
4 stalks celery, chopped
4 carrots, peeled and chopped
1 onion, chopped
1/4 c. quick-cooking barley,
    uncooked

8-oz. can tomato sauce
1 t. dried basil
2 cubes beef bouillon
3 potatoes, peeled and cubed
salt and pepper to taste

Combine broth and water in a large soup pot. Add celery, carrots, onion, barley, tomato sauce and basil; bring to a boil. Reduce heat; partially cover and simmer for 15 minutes. Add meatballs; cover and cook for 15 minutes. Add potatoes and cook until tender, about 20 minutes. Add salt and pepper to taste. Serves 6.

Meatballs:

1-1/2 lbs. ground beef
1/2 c. cooked rice
1 onion, finely chopped
1 egg, beaten

1/4 c. water
1 clove garlic, minced
salt and pepper to taste

Combine all ingredients in a large bowl; mix well. Shape into small meatballs.

Hang a flea-market-find window
shutter on the wall to hold
greeting cards, cookbooklets
or catalogs. Add a row of cup
hooks along the bottom to keep
potholders at your fingertips.

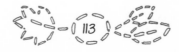

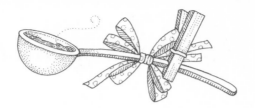

Grandma's Irish Soda Bread

Jennifer Savino
Joliet, IL

My grandma was 100 percent Irish and she knew how to make the best Irish soda bread around. Serve it warm from the oven, topped with a pat of butter...there's nothing better!

3 c. all-purpose flour
2/3 c. sugar
1 t. baking powder
1 t. baking soda
1 t. salt

1-1/2 c. raisins
2 eggs, beaten
1-3/4 c. buttermilk
2 T. butter, melted and slightly
   cooled

Sift dry ingredients together in a large bowl; stir in raisins and set aside. In a separate bowl, combine eggs, buttermilk and melted butter, blending well. Add egg mixture to flour mixture; stir until well mixed. Pour batter into two greased 9"x5" loaf pans. Bake at 350 degrees for one hour. Turn loaves out of pans and let cool on a wire rack. Makes 2 loaves.

Making butter is fun for kids. Pour a pint of heavy cream into a chilled wide-mouth jar, cap the jar tightly and take turns shaking until you see butter begin to form. When it's done, uncap the jar and rinse the butter lightly with cool water. Enjoy on warm, fresh-baked bread...yum!

Cozy Soups & Breads

PatPat's Pot of Soup

PatPat Storey
Cleveland, TN

This soup is quick & easy for friends and fellowship any night of the week! Just leave the slow cooker set on low until you get home from work. Serve with a basket of cornbread or corn chips...it's great either way!

15-1/2 oz. can chili with beans
15-1/2 oz. can chili without
   beans
15-1/4 oz. can corn

10-3/4 oz. can tomato soup
10-oz. can tomatoes with chiles
Garnish: shredded Cheddar
   cheese, sour cream

Combine all ingredients except garnish in a slow cooker. Cover and cook on low for 6 to 8 hours, until steaming hot. Serve soup portions garnished with cheese and sour cream. Serves 4.

A vintage-style oilcloth tablecloth with brightly colored fruit and flowers adds cheer to any dinner table. Its wipe-clean ease makes it oh-so practical for any meal of the day.

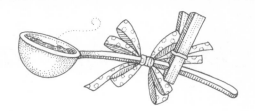

Spicy Sausage & Kale Soup

Sarah Gruber
Monroe, MI

*I love to make soup from scratch! When my youngest daughter was
expecting her first baby, I created this soup for her. She said it was so
good I should enter it in a contest! Serve it with warm crusty garlic
bread for a really satisfying meal.*

6 slices bacon, diced
1 onion, chopped
2 to 3 cloves garlic, minced
4 c. chicken broth
3 c. water or chicken broth
3 potatoes, peeled and diced
2 to 3 c. kale, chopped
14-1/2 oz. can diced tomatoes
   with chiles

15-oz. can chickpeas, drained
1/2 t. garlic powder
1/2 t. onion powder
1 lb. smoked pork sausage,
   halved lengthwise and sliced
   1/2-inch thick
1 c. whipping cream
salt and pepper to taste

In a large stockpot, cook bacon until crisp. Remove to paper towels
and drain, reserving 2 tablespoons drippings. Add onion and garlic;
sauté in reserved drippings until softened. Add broth, water or broth,
potatoes, kale, tomatoes with chiles, chickpeas, garlic powder and
onion powder. Bring to a boil; reduce heat and simmer until potatoes
and kale are cooked through, about 15 to 20 minutes. Meanwhile,
broil or fry sausage until browned; drain. Stir reserved bacon, sausage
and cream into soup. Heat gently for an additional 5 minutes; add salt
and pepper as needed. Makes 10 servings.

*There's nothing like soup for turning leftovers into a hot,
hearty meal. Keep a container in the freezer for extra
chopped vegetables, roast beef, shredded chicken or even
crispy bacon. When you have saved enough, just add a
couple of cans of broth and a can of diced tomatoes.
Simmer until everything blends together...scrumptious!*

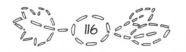

Farmstand Bacon-Corn Soup

Barbara Pache
Marshall, WI

*This creamy, savory soup really hits the spot in chilly weather!
Everyone who tries it wants the recipe, so I thought
I would share it with other **Gooseberry Patch** fans.*

1 butternut squash
12 slices bacon, diced
1 onion, chopped
1 stalk celery, chopped
1 T. all-purpose flour
14-1/2 oz. can chicken broth
2 14-3/4 oz. cans creamed corn

2 8-oz. cans corn, drained
1 pt. half-and-half
1 T. fresh parsley, minced
1-1/2 t. salt
1/2 t. pepper
Optional: sour cream

Place squash on an ungreased baking sheet. Bake at 375 degrees for
one hour. Cut in half; cool. Remove seeds with a spoon; scoop out
pulp and mash. Set aside. In a large saucepan over medium-high
heat, cook bacon until crisp. Remove bacon to paper towels, reserving
2 tablespoons drippings in saucepan. Sauté onion and celery until
tender. Stir in flour; blend well. Gradually stir in 6 cups squash and
remaining ingredients except sour cream; return crumbled bacon to
saucepan. Cook and stir over low heat until heated through.
Garnish with dollops of sour cream, if desired. Serves 8.

*Enjoy a favorite long-simmering recipe
more often...let a slow cooker do the work
for you! Brown and drain ground meat
first, then toss all ingredients into the
slow cooker. A soup that cooks
for 2 hours on the stovetop can
cook all day on the low setting
without burning or overcooking.*

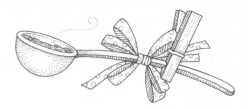

Yummy Carrot-Raisin Muffins

Nancy Haines
Hicksville, NY

This recipe for extra-moist muffins was a wonderful gift from
my secret pal! Substitute other flavors of cake mix too...
devil's food, orange and spice cake all make tasty muffins.

18-oz. pkg. carrot cake mix   1/3 c. golden raisins
15-oz. can pumpkin

Mix dry cake mix and pumpkin together to make a very thick batter.
Add raisins and mix well. Fill paper-lined muffin cups 2/3 full. Bake
at 400 degrees for 20 minutes, until muffins test done. Makes
one dozen.

An old-fashioned ice cream scoop isn't handy just for serving
up frozen treats. Use it for scooping muffin batter,
mashed potatoes and even jumbo meatballs...
you'll have perfect portions every time!

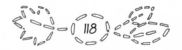

Butterfly Yeast Rolls

Janis Parr
Ontario, Canada

*I have been baking these delicious rolls for years and they are the best!
The rolls rise to perfection and are golden and flaky...
sure to delight family & friends.*

1 env. active dry yeast	1 t. salt
1/4 c. warm water	3-1/2 c. all-purpose flour,
1 c. milk	divided
1/4 c. sugar	1 egg, beaten
1/4 c. shortening	

In a small bowl, mix yeast with very warm water, 110 to
115 degrees; let stand for 5 minutes. Heat milk in a small saucepan
over low heat just until boiling; let cool slightly. In a large bowl,
combine milk, sugar, shortening and salt. Add 1-1/2 cups flour and
beat well. Beat in yeast mixture and egg. Gradually knead in
remaining flour to form a soft dough. Place in a greased bowl, turning
once. Cover and let rise in a warm place for 2 hours. Punch dough
down; turn out on a floured surface. Shape into 36 walnut-size balls;
place 3 balls in each cup of a greased muffin tin. Cover and let rise for
45 minutes. Bake at 400 degrees for 12 to 15 minutes, or until
golden. Makes one dozen.

*Give homebaked rolls and bread a mouthwatering golden
finish. Whisk together an egg yolk and a tablespoon of water
in a cup. Brush the mixture over the dough just before
sliding it into the oven...it's as simple as that.*

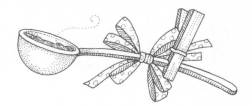

Crawfish-Corn Chowder

Becky Garrett
Richardson, TX

As displaced Cajuns from Lousiana now living in Texas, my family loves this chowder...it's a delicious reminder of home.

12-oz. pkg. bacon, crisply
   cooked, crumbled and
   drippings reserved
2 c. potatoes, peeled and diced
1 c. onion, diced
2 T. butter
2 pts. half-and-half

2 16-oz. cans creamed corn
1 T. Creole seasoning
Optional: 1 t. hot pepper sauce
1 lb. frozen crawfish tails or
   uncooked medium shrimp,
   peeled

Place 4 tablespoons reserved drippings in a soup pot. Sauté potatoes and onion for about 15 minutes, until golden. Stir in butter, half-and-half, corn, seasoning and hot sauce, if using. Add crumbled bacon to chowder. Cook over medium heat until potatoes are tender, 20 to 30 minutes. Add crawfish or shrimp and simmer for another 15 to 20 minutes; do not overcook. Serves 6 to 8.

Enamelware dishpans are so useful in the kitchen...don't pass them by at barn sales! They're perfect for mixing up company-size batches of bread dough, cookies, tossed salad, turkey dressing and so much more...even for serving popcorn on family movie night!

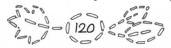

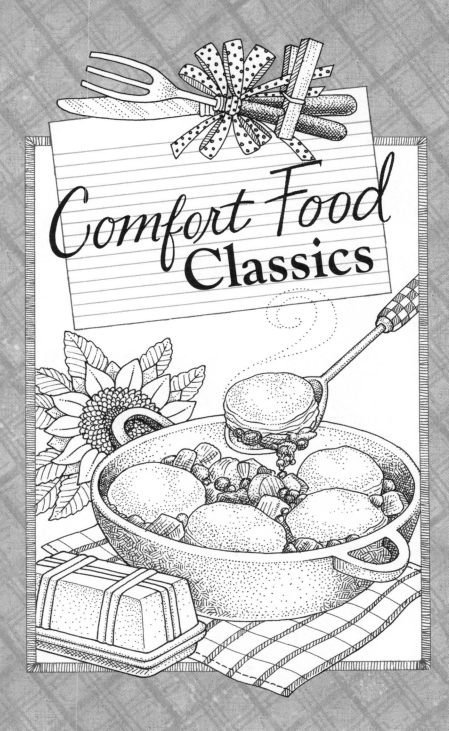

Comfort Food Classics

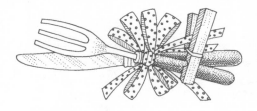

Angie's Pot Roast with Buttermilk Gravy

Lisa Stanish
Houston, TX

My best friend gave me this recipe and it is the absolute best roast I have ever had. Since then, I've shared the recipe with other friends countless times. Spoon the gravy from the slow cooker over mashed potatoes...pure comfort food!

3-lb. beef chuck roast
3 T. oil
1 onion, chopped
3 T. all-purpose flour
1 c. buttermilk

1 c. water
4 T. beef bouillon granules
1/2 t. dried thyme
1/2 t. pepper

In a large skillet over medium-high heat, brown roast in oil on all sides. Remove roast to a slow cooker, reserving drippings; top roast with onion and set aside. Add flour to drippings in skillet; cook and stir until brown. Add buttermilk, water, bouillon, thyme and pepper; cook and stir until thickened. Pour gravy over roast and onion in slow cooker. Cover and cook on low setting for 5 to 7 hours. Serves 6.

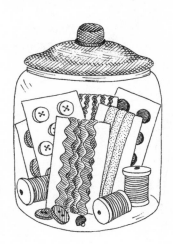

Whip up a pretty tablecloth in no time by using a pretty patterned sheet. Just cut it to fit the table, hem it and trim the edges with ribbon or rick rack.

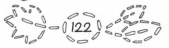

Comfort Food Classics

Shepherd's Pie

Donna Jenkins
Dayton, OH

*My husband, a self-proclaimed meat & potatoes man, always requests
this hearty one-dish favorite. The fact that it's simple to make
and easy on the wallet makes it that much better.*

1 onion, diced
1 to 2 t. oil
1 lb. ground beef
10-3/4 oz. can cream of
   mushroom soup
11-oz. can corn, drained

4 potatoes, peeled and cubed
1/4 c. milk
2 to 3 t. butter, sliced
salt and pepper to taste
3/4 c. shredded Cheddar or
   American cheese

In a skillet over medium heat, sauté onion in oil. Add ground beef and
cook until no longer pink; drain. In a large bowl, mix beef, soup and
corn; pour into a greased 8"x8" baking pan and set aside. Place
potatoes in a saucepan; cover with water. Boil over medium-high heat
until tender, about 10 minutes. Drain; add milk, butter, salt and
pepper to pan. Whip potatoes with a potato masher or electric mixer
and spread over beef mixture. Bake, covered, at 350 degrees for
30 minutes. Sprinkle with cheese and bake, uncovered, an additional
5 minutes. Serves 4.

*Pickle jars, penny candy jars and glass
pantry jars are so collectible! Use them
in your kitchen to hold everything from
pasta to cookies. They're great in
the craft room, too...buttons, bobbins
and spools will all be at home in
these old-time containers.*

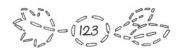

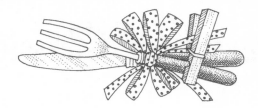

Company Baked Ziti

Colleen Leid
Narvon, PA

Oh-so simple to put together, yet everyone loves it!

1 lb. ground beef
1 lb. sweet Italian ground pork
　sausage
1 onion, chopped
2 26-1/2 oz. cans spaghetti
　sauce
16-oz. pkg. ziti pasta, cooked

6-oz. pkg. sliced provolone
　cheese
1 c. sour cream
1-1/2 c. shredded mozzarella
　cheese
Garnish: grated Parmesan
　cheese

Brown beef, sausage and onion together in a skillet; drain. Stir in sauce; reduce heat to low and simmer for 15 minutes. Layer in a greased 13"x9" baking pan as follows: half of pasta, provolone cheese, sour cream, half of sauce mixture, remaining pasta, mozzarella cheese and remaining sauce. Top with Parmesan cheese. Cover and bake at 350 degrees for 30 minutes, or until hot, bubbly and cheeses are melted. Serves 6 to 8.

The art of being happy lies in the power of
extracting happiness from common things.
-Henry Ward Beecher

Comfort Food Classics

Ted's Favorite Meatballs

Susie Backus
Gooseberry Patch

These are delicious...great served over buttered noodles.
Very different from your average meatball!

2 lbs. ground beef
1-1/2 c. bread crumbs
1-1/2 oz. pkg. onion soup mix
8-oz. container sour cream
1 egg, beaten
1/3 c. all-purpose flour

1 t. paprika
1/4 c. butter
10-3/4 oz. can cream of chicken
  soup
3/4 c. milk

Mix ground beef, crumbs, soup mix, sour cream and egg in a large bowl; form into walnut-size meatballs. Combine flour and paprika; roll meatballs in mixture. Melt butter in a large skillet over medium-high heat. Brown meatballs; drain. Blend soup and milk together and pour over browned meatballs. Cover and simmer for about 20 minutes. Makes 6 to 8 servings.

Making lots of mini meatballs? Grab a melon baller
and start scooping...you'll be done in record time!

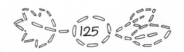

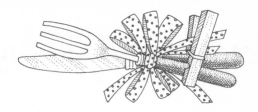

Saucy Pork Chop Scallop

Hope Yates
Wesley, AR

This recipe was handed down from my grandmother to my mother and then to me. It is very simple, yet is oh-so creamy and good.

4 pork chops
1 T. oil
salt and pepper to taste
10-3/4 oz. can cream of
   mushroom soup

1/2 c. sour cream
1/4 c. water
2 T. dried, minced onion
4 c. potatoes, peeled and thinly
   sliced

In a skillet over medium heat, brown pork chops in oil. Drain; sprinkle with salt and pepper. Blend together soup, sour cream, water, onion, potatoes and additional salt and pepper. Spread into a lightly greased 13"x9" baking pan. Top with browned pork chops. Cover; bake at 375 degrees for one hour and 15 minutes. Serves 4.

When pork chops are on the menu, sprinkle a little salt in your cast-iron skillet before adding the oil and the meat. You'll have less spattering and more flavorful pork chops.

Comfort Food Classics

Sweet-and-Sauerkraut Brats

Jo Ann

*I like to pop this into the slow cooker on Saturday mornings. Later,
when I get home from a day of barn sale-ing with friends,
I know a hearty meal will be ready to serve my family!*

1-1/2 to 2 lbs. bratwurst, cut
  into bite-size pieces
27-oz. can sauerkraut
4 tart apples, cored, peeled and
  chopped

1/4 c. onion, chopped
1/4 c. brown sugar, packed
1 t. caraway seed
4 to 6 hard rolls, split
Garnish: spicy mustard

Place bratwurst into a slow cooker. Toss together sauerkraut with
juice, apples, onion, brown sugar and caraway seed; spoon over
bratwurst. Cover and cook on low setting for 4 to 5 hours, stirring
occasionally. Fill rolls, using a slotted spoon. Serve with mustard on
the side. Makes 4 to 6 servings.

*Whip up some whimsical fridge magnets. Glue round cut-outs
from family photos into retro pop bottle caps. Add button
magnets to the back with a dab of hot glue.*

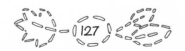

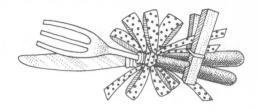

Easy Turkey & Dumplings

Tori Willis
Champaign, IL

*A scrumptious way to serve leftover roast turkey! Spoon into soup
plates and add a scattering of chopped fresh green parsley.*

1 lb. roast turkey breast, cubed
1/4 c. carrot, peeled and
   chopped
1/4 c. onion, chopped

1/4 c. celery, chopped
3 c. turkey or chicken broth
salt and pepper to taste
12-oz. tube refrigerated biscuits

Place turkey, vegetables and broth in a medium saucepan; bring to a
boil over medium heat. Reduce heat to low; simmer for 30 minutes,
adding salt and pepper to taste. Pat out biscuits together on a lightly
floured surface; cut into 2-inch by one-inch pieces. Drop biscuit pieces
into the simmering broth. Cook over low heat for 10 to 15 minutes,
until dumplings are done. Serve ladled into bowls. Makes 4 to
6 servings.

*Add some whimsy to plain-Jane window shades...
simply use fabric glue to attach vintage sewing trim
like rick rack or pompom fringe along the edge.*

Comfort Food Classics

Fried Chicken & Milk Gravy

Darrell Lawry
Kissimmee, FL

My family likes dark meat, but if you prefer, you can substitute chicken breasts, sliced in half lengthwise so they'll cook quicker.

2/3 c. plus 1/4 c. all-purpose
  flour, divided
1 t. dried thyme
1/2 t. onion powder
1/2 t. seasoning salt
1/2 t. pepper, divided

8 chicken thighs or drumsticks
2/3 c. buttermilk
2 to 4 T. oil
1 t. chicken bouillon granules
1-1/2 c. milk

Combine 2/3 cup flour, thyme, onion powder, salt and 1/4 teaspoon pepper in a large plastic zipping bag. Add chicken to bag, one or 2 pieces at a time; shake to coat well. Dip chicken into buttermilk; return to bag and shake to coat. Heat oil in a large skillet over medium heat. Add chicken and sauté for 15 minutes, turning to cook evenly until golden. Reduce heat to medium-low. Cook, uncovered, for an additional 35 to 40 minutes, until chicken is tender and juices run clear when pierced. Remove chicken to paper towels, reserving drippings; cover chicken to keep warm. Stir bouillon, remaining flour and remaining pepper into skillet drippings, scraping up any browned bits. Add milk. Cook and stir over medium heat until thickened and bubbly; cook and stir one additional minute. Serve hot gravy over chicken. Serves 4.

Nobody likes lumpy gravy! If the gravy has lumps, pour it through a mesh tea strainer just before serving time.

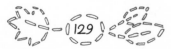

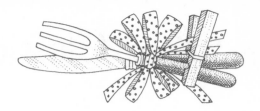

Baked Ham in Peach Sauce

JoAnna Nicoline-Haughey
Berwyn, PA

This ham with its fruity sauce is equally scrumptious served hot at a holiday dinner or cold at a summer picnic.

5-lb. fully-cooked ham	10-oz. jar apricot preserves
1 t. whole cloves	1 c. dry sherry or apple juice
2 16-oz. cans sliced peaches,	1 t. orange zest
drained	1/2 t. allspice

Place ham in an ungreased 13"x9" baking pan. Score surface of ham in a diamond pattern; insert cloves. Combine remaining ingredients in a blender or food processor. Process until smooth and pour over ham. Cover ham with aluminum foil. Bake at 325 degrees for 30 minutes, basting occasionally with sauce. Uncover and bake for an additional 30 minutes; continue to baste. Remove ham to a serving platter; slice and serve with sauce from pan. May be served hot or cold. Makes 10 servings.

Don't overlook Grandma's ironstone pitcher & bowl set when setting out a dinner buffet! Fill the pitcher with refreshing ice water and lemon slices...put the bowl to work serving up a party-size portion of your favorite salad or side.

Comfort Food Classics

Best-Ever Country Ribs

Jill Nikunen
Kalispell, MT

With just 3 ingredients, this is the easiest BBQ rib recipe ever! We like to serve it with twice-baked potatoes and a crisp green salad for an easy everyday meal that's anything but ordinary.

1 onion, cut into wedges
3 lbs. boneless country-style
   pork ribs, cut into 2-inch
   cubes

18-oz. bottle barbecue sauce

Place onion wedges in the bottom of a lightly greased slow cooker. Place ribs on top of onion. Cover and cook on high for one hour. Stir; pour barbecue sauce over ribs. Cover; reduce heat and cook on low for an additional 4 hours, until ribs are tender. Serves 4 to 6.

Give a new white tablecloth a warm vintage look with tea-dyeing. Fill a large pot with water, bring to a boil and steep 8 to 10 teabags. Add the prewashed, damp tablecloth to the pot and simmer for at least 30 minutes, until it's the tint you like. Rinse, dry and enjoy.

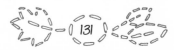

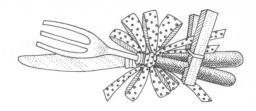

Country Noodle Dish

Christine Waterbury
Sheboygan, WI

Serve with a crisp tossed salad and piping-hot garlic bread.

1 lb. ground beef or turkey
1 onion, chopped
Optional: 2 T. green pepper,
  chopped
11-oz. can corn, drained

2 10-3/4 oz. cans tomato soup
8-oz. pkg. medium egg noodles,
  cooked
1/2 to 3/4 c. water
salt and pepper to taste

In a skillet over medium heat, brown meat with onion and green pepper, if using. Drain; stir in corn. Stir in soup, cooked noodles and water to desired consistency. Add salt and pepper to taste. Heat through and serve. Makes 4 to 6 servings.

Look for colorful old-fashioned cut flowers like zinnias and dwarf sunflowers at farmers' markets and even your neighborhood supermarket. Arrange a generous bunch in a tall stoneware crock for a cheery centerpiece.

Comfort Food Classics

Baked Potatoes & Chicken Sauce

*Karie Rittenour
Gooseberry Patch*

*A few simple ingredients turn baked potatoes into a filling,
comforting meal.*

4 baking potatoes
1 to 2 t. oil
2 5-oz. cans chicken, drained
   and flaked
1 c. sour cream

1/2 c. mayonnaise
4 t. milk
1/2 t. seasoned salt
1/4 t. pepper
Optional: fresh parsley, chopped

Pierce skins of potatoes several times with a fork; rub oil lightly
over potatoes. Bake at 350 degrees for about one hour, until tender.
Combine remaining ingredients in a small saucepan over low heat.
Heat through, stirring occasionally, until hot and bubbly. Slice baked
potatoes in half lengthwise; place each potato on a plate. Spoon
chicken mixture over potatoes. Garnish with a sprinkle of parsley, if
desired. Makes 4 servings.

*Tiny china plates called butter pats can often be found at
tag sales. Use them as whimsical teabag holders...little girls
would love to play with them as doll dishes too. So sweet!*

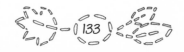

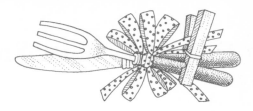

Cheesy Macaroni Skillet

Donna Scheletsky
Baden, PA

Even if you're just arriving home from work, you can serve your family
this stovetop casserole...it's easy & quick to fix. They'll love it!

8-oz. pkg. elbow macaroni,
   uncooked
1/2 lb. bacon, diced

14-1/2 oz. can diced tomatoes
8-oz. can tomato sauce
1 c. shredded Cheddar cheese

Measure out 2 cups macaroni and cook according to package
directions; drain. Reserve remaining uncooked macaroni for another
recipe. Fry bacon in a large skillet until crisp. Drain, leaving about
one tablespoon drippings in skillet. Add tomatoes with juice, tomato
sauce and cooked macaroni. Simmer over low heat until hot and
bubbly. Add cheese; place lid on skillet and let stand until cheese is
melted. Serves 4.

When making a favorite casserole, it's easy to make a double
batch. After baking, let the extra casserole cool and tuck
it in the freezer...ready to share with a new mother,
carry to a potluck or reheat on a busy night at home.

Comfort Food Classics

Grandma's Ham Potpie

Eva Drummond
Timberville, VA

My grandma used to make the very best country ham potpie...not the crust-topped casserole, but rather a kind of Pennsylvania Dutch dish with noodle dumplings. She made her own dough from scratch. Now I use ready-made frozen dumplings. It is quick & easy to feed a crowd with this recipe. My grandchildren request this a lot.

2 10-oz. pkgs. cooked ham, cubed
6 qts. water
6 potatoes, peeled and diced

2 12-oz. pkgs. frozen potpie dumplings or frozen homestyle egg noodles
salt and pepper to taste
Garnish: chopped onion

Combine ham and water in a large saucepan. Simmer over medium heat for 30 minutes. Add potatoes and cook for an additional 15 minutes. Increase heat so water is boiling and add frozen dumplings or noodles, one at a time. Stir in salt and pepper to taste. Reduce heat and simmer for 15 minutes. Stir frequently to avoid sticking to pan. If mixture gets too thick, add a little hot water. Garnish servings with chopped onion. Serves 8 to 10.

Tie ruffled vintage aprons onto the backs of kitchen chairs for a sweet welcome to a country-style supper.

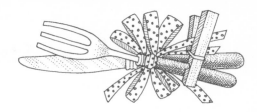

Poor Man's Meal

JoAnne Fajack
Youngstown, OH

This recipe brings back a lot of memories for me. It was made by my dad when the Second World War was going on. Times were hard...food was hard to get and many things weren't available at all. Dad grew the potatoes in our garden as well as the onions and parsley. We would eat it with bread that the lady next door had baked in an outdoor oven. This will feed around 6 people very well.

1 T. oil
1-lb. pkg. hot dogs, sliced
   1/2-inch thick
1 onion, chopped
salt, pepper, Italian seasoning
   and dried parsley to taste

6 to 8 potatoes, peeled and
   sliced 1/2-inch thick
paprika to taste

Place oil in a frying pan over medium heat. Add hot dogs and onion; cook until lightly browned. Add water to cover and bring to a boil. Add seasonings to taste. Reduce heat and simmer for about 20 minutes. Add potatoes and enough paprika to give the whole mixture a red color. Cook until potatoes are tender, adding a little more water if needed. Add additional seasonings to taste. Serves 6.

Embellish a small notebook with seed packet clippings... oh-so useful for making shopping lists or keeping schedules. Tie up a stack with rick rack or ribbon for gift giving.

136

Comfort Food Classics

Becky's BBQ Beef for a Crowd

Becky Hall
Belton, MO

This is a very flexible recipe...just the thing for a take-it-easy cookout. It holds well in a slow cooker, freezes well and reheats well in the microwave. I've used this recipe for large groups, cooking 12 to 15 pounds of meat at a time, doubling the other ingredients and increasing the baking time to 6 hours. The smoke flavoring adds so much, so don't omit it!

5 to 6-lb. beef chuck roast
1/2 to 1 t. salt
1/2 to 1 t. pepper
2 14-1/2 oz. cans stewed or
   crushed tomatoes

2 onions, chopped
3 T. sugar
2 T. smoke-flavored cooking
   sauce
Optional: vinegar to taste

Place roast in an ungreased large roasting pan; sprinkle with salt and pepper to taste. Mix remaining ingredients. If mixture is too sweet, add vinegar, about one teaspoon at a time. Pour over roast. Cover and bake at 325 degrees for 4 hours, basting occasionally. Makes 10 to 12 servings.

Thrifty country cooks were used to putting away fresh meat in large amounts for later use. Why not do as they did and save money on meals? Stock up at supermarket sales on large packages of ground beef, chuck steak, chicken or pork chops, then repackage into recipe-size portions before freezing.

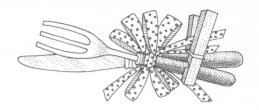

Tuna & Noodle Casserole

Marcie Graham
Sulphur, LA

Everybody's favorite comfort food.

8-oz. pkg. wide egg noodles,
   cooked
2 6-oz. cans tuna, drained
10-3/4 oz. can cream of
   mushroom soup
1 c. milk

1 c. shredded Cheddar cheese
1 tomato, sliced
salt and pepper to taste
3/4 c. to 1 c. seasoned dry bread
   crumbs

Mix cooked noodles with tuna, soup, milk and cheese. Transfer to a buttered 9"x9" baking pan. Arrange tomato slices on top; sprinkle with salt and pepper. Top with bread crumbs. Bake, uncovered, for 15 minutes at 375 degrees, until hot and bubbly. Serves 6.

First aid for old casserole dishes with baked-on food spatters!
Mix equal amounts of cream of tartar and white vinegar into
a paste. Spread onto the dish and let stand for 30 minutes
to an hour. The spatters will wash off easily.

Comfort Food Classics

Grandma Great's Chicken Casserole
Judy Taylor
Butler, MO

This hearty casserole was my mother-in-law's special dish. Whether it's a family gathering or church social, everyone loves it!

4 to 5 boneless, skinless
  chicken breasts
1 green pepper, chopped
2 onions, chopped
1/2 c. oil
4-oz. can sliced mushrooms,
  drained

Optional: 2-oz. jar sliced
  pimentos, drained
8-oz. pkg. pasteurized process
  cheese spread, shredded
16-oz. pkg. thin spaghetti,
  cooked

Place chicken in a large saucepan; add water to cover. Simmer over medium heat until tender, about 30 minutes. Remove chicken and cool. Drain saucepan, reserving 2 cups broth. In the same pan, cook pepper and onions in oil; drain. Stir in reserved broth, mushrooms and pimentos, if desired; bring to a simmer. Chop chicken and add along with cheese and spaghetti. Transfer to a lightly greased 2-quart casserole dish. Cover and bake at 350 degrees for 30 minutes. Uncover; continue baking until lightly golden on top and liquid is absorbed, 20 to 30 minutes. Makes 6 to 8 servings.

Blue Willow is a classic vintage china pattern, so soothing to the eye...why not start a collection of pieces from tag sales and thrift shops? Whether they're fine porcelain or treasures from the 5 & dime, your mix & match finds are sure to blend together.

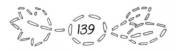

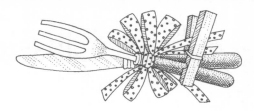

Aunt B's Chicken Tetrazzini

Bryna Dunlap
Muskogee, OK

*This makes two large trays of cheesy, chickeny pasta...perfect
for any church gathering when a covered dish is requested.*

8 c. chicken broth
2 yellow onions, chopped
2 green peppers, chopped
16-oz. pkg. angel hair pasta,
   uncooked
2 lbs. boneless, skinless chicken
   breasts, cooked
2 4-oz. cans sliced mushrooms,
   drained

2 c. butter
1-1/2 c. all-purpose flour
4 c. milk
6 c. pasteurized process cheese
   spread, cubed
Garnish: bread crumbs

In a large stockpot over medium heat, simmer broth, onions and
peppers until boiling. Add pasta and cook as directed; do not drain.
Add chicken and mushrooms; set aside. In a medium saucepan over
medium-low heat, combine butter, flour, milk and cheese. Cook and
stir until thickened; add to broth mixture and combine well. Pour into
two lightly greased deep 13"x9" baking pans and top with bread
crumbs. Bake, uncovered, at 350 degrees for 30 minutes, or until hot
and bubbly. Makes about 12 servings.

*Don't pass up large, old-fashioned enamelware stockpots at
tag sales. They're just the right size for family-size portions
of stew, soup and other favorites...and, indispensable
for simmering chicken & noodles.*

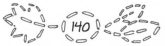

Comfort Food Classics

Skillet Turkey Stroganoff

Tammy Woodall
Glasgow, KY

With ground turkey and whole-wheat noodles, this is a yummy, healthy take on beef stroganoff. Use lowfat sour cream if you like.

1 lb. ground turkey, browned
   and drained
10-3/4 oz. can cream of
   mushroom soup

1 c. sour cream
1/2 c. milk
cooked whole-wheat egg
   noodles

Combine all ingredients except noodles in a skillet over medium heat. Cook until thickened, stirring occasionally, about 15 minutes. Serve spooned over cooked noodles. Serves 4.

You're sure to find lots of sweet old-fashioned picture books in small-town thrift stores. Keep them piled in a basket for wee visitors to enjoy.

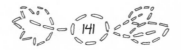

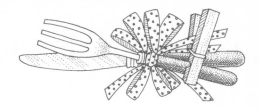

Tomato Beef Stew

Michelle Sheridan
Gooseberry Patch

Ladle over fluffy biscuits...yum!

4 lbs. stew beef, cubed
16-oz. pkg. frozen mixed
   vegetables
29-oz. can tomato sauce

1/4 c. onion, chopped
1-1/2 oz. pkg. beef stew
   seasoning mix
1 T. Worcestershire sauce

Combine all ingredients in a slow cooker; stir well. Cover and cook on low setting for 9 to 10 hours, or on high setting for 4 to 5 hours. Makes 10 to 12 servings.

Make a double recipe of your favorite comfort food and invite neighbors over for supper...what a great way to get to know them better. Keep it simple with a tossed salad, warm bakery bread and brownies for dessert...it's all about food and fellowship!

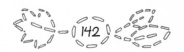

Comfort Food Classics

Paprika Beef & Noodles

Joan White
Malvern, PA

Choose sweet Hungarian paprika for the most robust flavor.

2 to 2-1/2 lbs. boneless beef
   chuck roast, cubed
2 onions, chopped
3 T. butter
8-oz. can tomato sauce
2 t. Worcestershire sauce
2 t. sugar
2 t. paprika

1-1/2 t. caraway seed
1 t. dill weed
1/8 t. garlic powder
1 to 2 t. salt
1/4 t. pepper
8-oz. container sour cream
cooked egg noodles

In a Dutch oven over medium-high heat, cook beef and onions in butter until meat is browned. Add sauces, sugar and seasonings; bring to a boil. Reduce heat to low; cover and simmer for 1-3/4 to 2 hours, or until beef is tender. Remove from heat; stir in sour cream. Serve over cooked noodles. Serves 4 to 6.

Every farmhouse kitchen should have a wooden tasting spoon by the stovetop! With a spoon at each end and a groove in the handle, the design allows hot food to cool slightly before being sampled by the cook. If you're lucky, you may find a hand-carved example at a craft fair.

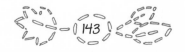

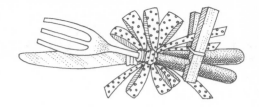

Brown Sugar Ham

Melissa Dawn
Kennewick, WA

*For the prettiest presentation, score the ham in a diamond pattern
before brushing on the sweet & savory glaze.*

4 to 5-lb. fully cooked ham	1/3 c. honey
1 c. brown sugar, packed	1 T. dried rosemary
1/2 c. spicy mustard	1 T. ground cumin

Place ham in an ungreased large roaster pan. Mix together remaining
ingredients and spread over ham. Bake, covered, at 375 degrees for
35 to 40 minutes. Uncover and bake for an additional 10 to
15 minutes. Let stand briefly before slicing. Serves 8 to 10.

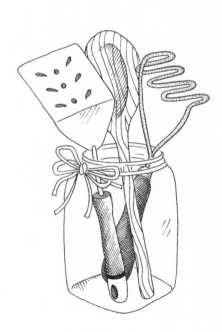

*Fill a large canning jar or an enamelware pitcher with vintage
red-handled kitchen utensils...instant nostalgia!*

Comfort Food Classics

Cheryl's Country-Style Ribs

Cheryl Tesar
DeWitt, NE

A family favorite...so delicious, there are rarely any leftovers!
I like to serve it with golden cornbread, a pot of
baked beans and sweet baked apples.

7 to 8 lbs. country-style pork
   ribs, sliced into serving-size
   portions

salt to taste
2 onions, sliced
1/2 c. brown sugar, packed

Place ribs in an ungreased large roaster pan; sprinkle lightly with salt. Top ribs with onion slices, brown sugar and 3/4 of Barbecue Sauce. Cover and bake at 350 degrees for 2 hours. Uncover and add remaining sauce. Increase oven to 400 degrees; bake for an additional 30 minutes. Makes 12 to 15 servings.

Barbecue Sauce:

2 c. catsup
1 c. water
1/2 c. sugar
1/2 c. vinegar
1/2 c. Worcestershire sauce

2 T. smoke-flavored cooking
   sauce
1 t. garlic powder
1 t. salt

Combine all ingredients and mix well. Keep refrigerated.

Relax and serve your next
dinner party family-style...
set large platters of food
right on the table so guests
can help themselves.

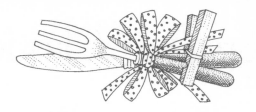

Roast Chicken & Vegetables

Beckie Butcher
Elgin, IL

This is my own creation from about 10 years ago, when I discovered my true love of cooking. Every time I serve this, I get rave reviews from some of the best cooks in my family...it's quite an ego booster!

3 to 4-lb. roasting chicken
salt and pepper to taste
1 onion, chopped

2 carrots, peeled and chopped
3 stalks celery, chopped
1 tomato, sliced

Place chicken in an ungreased roasting pan. Sprinkle with salt and pepper to taste. Fill loosely with Sage Stuffing, allowing room for stuffing to expand. Place onion, carrots and celery around chicken; add enough water to cover vegetables. Cover; bake at 350 degrees for one hour. Add tomato; cover again and bake for 30 additional minutes. Uncover to allow browning; bake for a final 30 minutes, until juices run clear. Place chicken on a platter and carve. Serve stuffing and vegetables separately. Serves 4 to 6.

Sage Stuffing:

14-oz. pkg. sage-flavored
   stuffing mix
2 to 2-1/2 c. boiling water
1 egg, beaten

1 onion, chopped
1 stalk celery, chopped
Optional: dried sage to taste

Place stuffing mix in a large bowl. Add water to desired consistency; toss to moisten. Stir in remaining ingredients until well blended.

Turn leftover bread stuffing into a tasty side dish, or toss in some browned sausage to make it a main dish. Simply spoon stuffing into green peppers or squash halves and bake at 350 degrees until heated through and tender.

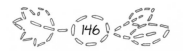

Comfort Food Classics

Delicious Drumsticks

Renae Scheiderer
Beallsville, OH

*This is a good recipe that was given to me when I was first married
and just learning how to cook. I still enjoy fixing it!*

1/2 c. all-purpose flour
1/2 t. paprika
1 t. salt

1/4 t. pepper
1/4 c. butter, melted and cooled
1-1/2 lbs. chicken drumsticks

Mix flour and seasonings in a shallow bowl; place melted butter in a
separate shallow bowl. Dip drumsticks into butter; roll in flour mixture
to coat. Arrange in an ungreased 8"x8" baking pan. Bake, uncovered,
at 425 degrees until done, about 50 minutes. Makes 4 to 6 servings.

Keep a large shaker of seasoned flour close at hand for
sprinkling on pork chops and chicken before frying.
A good mix is one cup flour, 1/4 cup seasoned salt
and one tablespoon pepper.

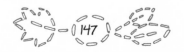

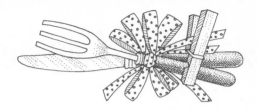

Country Chicken & Dumplin's

Jennifer Jones
McDonough, GA

My mother-in-law always made this for me when I came to visit.
It always warmed me up and made me feel so cozy.
It's great with fried okra!

4 to 5-lb. chicken
2 14-1/2 oz. cans chicken broth
3 c. water
10-3/4 oz. can cream of chicken
  soup

2 10-oz. tubes refrigerated
  biscuits, quartered
salt and pepper to taste

Place chicken in a large pot; add broth and water. Bring to a boil;
reduce heat and simmer for about 45 minutes, until chicken is done.
Remove chicken from pot, reserving broth; let chicken cool for
30 minutes. Add soup to reserved broth in pot; stir to mix over
medium heat. Pull chicken from bones and return to the pot. Add
biscuit pieces. Simmer for 15 minutes, or until dumplings have puffed
up, stirring occasionally. Add salt and pepper to taste. Serves 5.

A soup tureen adds old-fashioned flair to any dinner table or
buffet. Warm it up before ladling in homemade chicken
& dumplings or beef stew and it will stay hot longer.
Just fill with hot water, let stand for a few minutes,
pour out the water and it's ready!

Comfort Food Classics

Homestyle Beef Stew

Sophia Graves
Okeechobee, FL

This recipe has such wonderful memories for me. My mom would only make this on the coldest of winter days. We never knew when that would be, but I knew when I walked up to the house that Mom had something good cooking in the kitchen by the steam on the windows. When I opened the front door, the aroma would just envelope me... I could hardly wait until dinner!

2 to 3-lb. beef roast, cut into
    bite-size pieces
salt and pepper to taste
1 c. all-purpose flour
1/2 c. olive oil, divided
5 c. beef broth
5 cloves garlic

9 new redskin potatoes,
    quartered
1 lb. baby carrots
1/2 to 1 lb. mushrooms,
    quartered
1/2 to 1 c. pearl onions
10-oz. pkg. frozen peas

Sprinkle beef with salt and pepper; coat with flour. Spray a large pot with non-stick vegetable spray. Working in two batches, brown beef in oil over medium heat; remove beef from pot and set aside. Add broth to pot, scraping up all the browned bits in the bottom. Return meat to pot; add garlic and additional salt and pepper to taste. Bring to a boil for 15 minutes. Reduce heat, cover and simmer. After one hour, stir and cover again. Check meat for doneness after 2 hours; add potatoes, carrots, mushrooms and onions. Cover, increase heat to medium and cook for 30 minutes more, or until vegetables are tender. Remove from heat; discard garlic and stir in peas. Cover; let stand for about 20 minutes until peas are heated through. Makes 8 to 10 servings.

Quick & easy farmhouse napkin rings! Glue a charm or button to a little grapevine ring and slip in a cloth napkin.

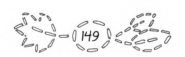

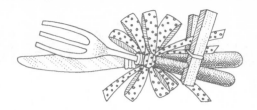

Roast Chicken Dijon

Kendall Hale
Lynn, MA

This recipe is so simple and scrumptious...we love it! Sometimes I'll make extra sauce to toss with redskin potatoes and tuck them around the chicken for a meal-in-one.

3 to 4-lb. roasting chicken
1/4 c. Dijon mustard
2 T. lemon juice

1 T. olive oil
salt and pepper to taste

Place chicken on a rack in an ungreased roasting pan. Mix mustard, lemon juice and oil in a small bowl. Brush mixture over chicken; sprinkle with salt and pepper. Bake, uncovered, at 425 degrees for 40 minutes, or until chicken juices run clear when pierced with a fork. Let stand for several minutes before slicing. Serves 4 to 6.

Don't toss the bones from a roast chicken! Turn it into delicious broth...it's oh-so-simple with a slow cooker. Combine the bones with a big handful of chopped onion, carrots and celery. Add 6 cups water, cover and cook on low setting for 8 to 10 hours. Strain, refrigerate and skim fat, then freeze in one-cup portions. They'll be ready to use in your favorite recipes.

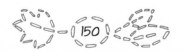

Comfort Food Classics

Brunswick Chicken Bake

Jill Valentine
Jackson, TN

My husband loves a big kettle of down-home Brunswick stew, so when I found this casserole-style recipe, I knew he'd like it too. For a really traditional dish, sometimes I'll substitute a package of frozen sliced okra for one of the packages of succotash.

2 T. oil
2-1/2 lbs. chicken
1 onion, chopped
2 T. all-purpose flour
.9-oz. pkg. Italian salad
   dressing mix

14-1/2 oz. can diced tomatoes
   with green peppers and
   onions
1 bay leaf
2 10-oz. pkgs. frozen
   succotash, thawed

Heat oil in a large skillet over medium-high heat. Brown chicken on all sides, about 15 minutes. Drain, reserving 2 tablespoons drippings in skillet. Arrange chicken in an ungreased 13"x9" baking pan and set aside. Add onion to skillet; sauté until tender. Stir in flour and salad dressing mix. Add tomatoes and bay leaf; cook and stir until bubbly. Stir in succotash and heat through. Pour skillet mixture over chicken; cover with aluminum foil. Bake at 350 degrees for one hour, until chicken juices run clear when pierced with a fork. Discard bay leaf before serving. Serves 4.

A toy-size little red wagon filled with seasonal flowers
makes a nostalgic, farmhouse centerpiece.

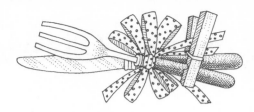

Chicken & Dumplings

Julie Kline
Kewanna, IN

Our farm family enjoys this after a long day of harvest or beef cattle chores. It's a hearty meal paired with coleslaw and a dish of fruit.

2 c. cooked chicken, chopped
8 c. chicken broth
1 c. potatoes, peeled and diced
1 c. celery, chopped
1/2 c. carrots, peeled and diced

1/4 c. onion, minced
1 c. frozen peas
1/4 t. dried parsley
pepper to taste

Combine chicken, broth, potatoes, celery, carrots and onion in a Dutch oven. Bring to a boil over medium heat while preparing Potpie Dumplings. Drop dumplings into boiling broth. Cover and cook for 15 minutes over medium heat. Stir in frozen peas, parsley and pepper to taste. Cook for about 2 minutes, until peas are cooked through, and serve. Makes 6 to 8 servings.

Potpie Dumplings:

2 c. all-purpose flour
2 t. salt
2 T. butter, chilled

2 eggs, beaten
1/4 c. water

Combine flour and salt. Cut in butter with a pastry blender or 2 forks. Stir in eggs and water until combined. Knead on a floured surface for 2 minutes. Roll out thinly on a floured surface; cut into one-inch squares.

Throw an apron party! Invite your best girlfriends to tie on their frilliest vintage aprons and join you in the kitchen to whip up a favorite dish together. It's a fun way to catch up with everyone.

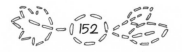

Comfort Food Classics

Schinken Nudeln

Christine Middleton
Nicholson, PA

German ham and noodles...delicious with or without catsup.

2 T. olive oil
2 T. butter
1 onion, finely chopped
1/2 lb. cooked ham, cut into
   bite-size cubes
Optional: 1/4 lb. bacon, chopped
16-oz. pkg. spaghetti, cooked

salt and pepper to taste
1/4 t. dried oregano
1/4 t. dried basil
1/2 t. dried parsley
2 eggs, beaten
Optional: catsup

Heat oil and butter in a large skillet. Sauté onion until transparent; add ham and bacon, if using. Cook until meat is done; quickly stir in seasonings. Transfer ham mixture to a separate dish. Add cooked spaghetti to skillet; top with ham mixture. Fry until spaghetti turns golden on bottom. Stir from bottom, mixing everything together; fry until heated through. Just before serving, pour in eggs; stir over low heat to mix and cook eggs, 3 to 5 minutes. Serve with catsup, if desired. Makes 6 servings.

If you're short on table space, an old-fashioned wooden ironing board makes a sturdy sideboard. Just adjust it to a convenient height, add a pretty table runner and set out the food... come & get it!

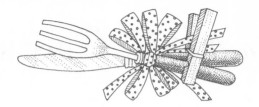

Honey & Brown Sugar Meatloaf

Lea Ann Burwell
Charles Town, WV

My father-in-law raises honeybees and shares the honey with us. One day I experimented with it and this has become my husband's favorite meatloaf recipe. It is simply delicious. He also likes to use the leftovers to make hot meatloaf sandwiches the next day...yum!

2-1/2 lbs. ground beef
1 sleeve saltine crackers,
   crushed
1 egg, beaten

2 c. catsup, divided
1/2 c. honey
1/2 c. brown sugar, packed

Mix ground beef, cracker crumbs, egg and 1/2 cup catsup in a large bowl until thoroughly mixed. Shape into a loaf and place in an ungreased 13"x9" baking pan. Spread 1/2 cup catsup on top of loaf. Bake at 350 degrees for one hour and 15 minutes. Mix honey, brown sugar and remaining catsup together with a whisk. Remove meatloaf from oven and pour glaze over the top. Place meatloaf under the broiler until glaze starts to bubble. Let cool slightly before slicing. Serves 6 to 8.

Often, for the tastiest country cooking, no fancy tools are needed...dig right in and mix that meatloaf with your hands!

Comfort Food Classics

Flat Meatballs & Gravy

Susan Harford
Pleasanton, CA

My husband's mother, Arlene Harford, used to make this recipe for her children. David has in turn made it for our three girls, Jennifer, Liz and Stephanie. It continues to be a family favorite.

2 lbs. ground beef round
1 egg, beaten
1/2 c. milk
1 T. all-purpose flour
1 t. salt
1/2 t. pepper

Optional: 1 onion, diced
2 T. butter
10-3/4 oz. can cream of
   mushroom soup
cooked rice

Mix all ingredients except butter, soup and rice together in a large bowl; set aside. Melt butter in a frying pan over medium heat. Scoop beef mixture into frying pan with an ice cream scoop; use spoon to shape into flattened meatballs. Brown over medium heat, turning several times. Remove meatballs to an ungreased 2-quart casserole dish; reserve drippings in pan. Stir soup into drippings; pour over meatballs. Bake, uncovered, at 350 degrees for 30 minutes. Serve over cooked rice. Serves 8.

Don't have enough dining-table chairs for when everyone gets together? Pick up mismatched tag-sale chairs for a song... paint them in a country color like barn red or robin's egg blue. Stencil on stars, hearts or even family members' names for a sweet personal touch.

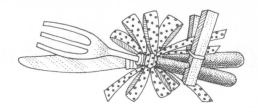

Easy Baked Chicken

Patti Walker
Mocksville, NC

This is a yummy quick meal for hurried evenings when I'm running the children back & forth from tennis matches or football practice. I like to put this dish in to bake while I run out to do carpool...when we get home, it's ready to serve! I round out the meal with steamed green beans.

6 frozen boneless, skinless
   chicken breasts
10-3/4 oz. can cream of
   mushroom soup
10-3/4 oz. can cream of onion
   soup

1/2 c. milk
2 T. margarine, diced
cooked egg noodles

Arrange frozen chicken in a single layer in a lightly greased 13"x9" baking pan. Mix soups and milk together; spread mixture over chicken, covering chicken well. Dot chicken with margarine. Cover baking pan with aluminum foil so that it is sealed well. Bake at 350 degrees for one to 1-1/2 hours, until cooked through. Serve chicken over egg noodles; spoon sauce from pan over all. Serves 4 to 6.

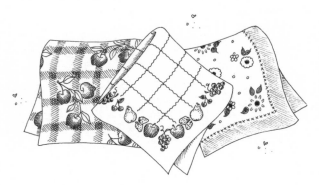

A simple trick to add down-home flavor to a roasting chicken. Cover it with several thick slices of hickory-smoked country bacon before popping it into the oven.

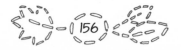

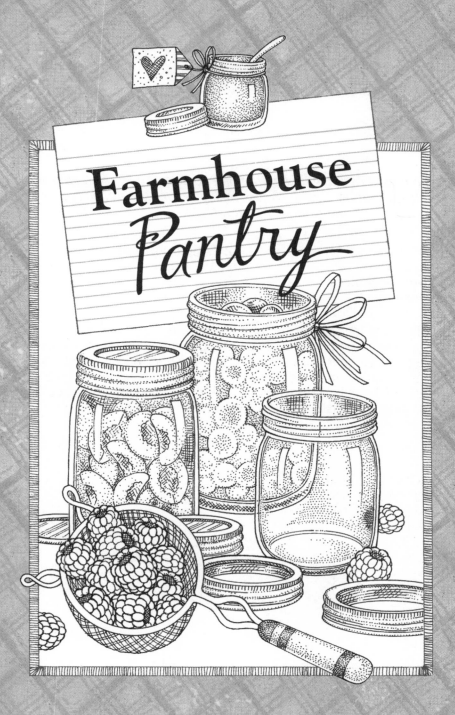

Farmhouse
Pantry

Mom's Hot Bacon Dressing

Jacqueline Kurtz
Wernersville, PA

My mom used to make this all the time to drizzle over fresh endive...
it's a country classic. This dressing is very good added to
homemade hot potato salad too.

4 slices bacon
2 T. sugar
2 T. all-purpose flour
1 egg, beaten

2 T. cider vinegar
1/4 c. water
3/4 c. milk

In a skillet over medium heat, cook bacon until crisp. Remove bacon and drain, reserving drippings in skillet. In a small bowl, mix sugar, flour, egg and vinegar until smooth. Stir in water and milk and add to drippings. Crumble bacon and return to skillet. Cook over medium-low heat until thickened. More water or milk may be added until dressing reaches desired consistency. Serve warm. Makes 4 servings.

When frying bacon, it's easy to prepare a few extra slices to
tuck into the fridge. Combine with juicy slices of sun-ripened
tomato, frilly lettuce and creamy mayonnaise for a fresh
BLT sandwich...tomorrow's lunch is ready in a jiffy!

Farmhouse *Pantry*

Sweet-and-Sour Dressing

Lori Graham
Pittsfield, PA

*A friend shared this recipe for an easy, light dressing. It's tasty
on taco salads as well as on tossed green salads.*

6 T. cider vinegar
1 c. brown sugar, packed
1 T. sugar

1/4 c. oil
1/4 t. garlic salt

In a small saucepan over low heat, cook and stir all ingredients until
sugars are dissolved. Cool; pour into a covered container. May be kept
refrigerated for up to 2 weeks. Makes 10 servings.

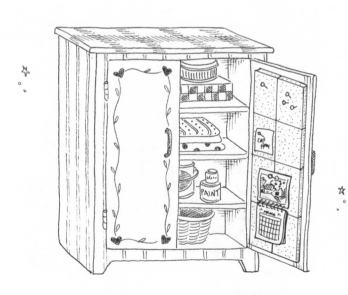

Line the inside of a kitchen cabinet door with self-stick cork
tiles. It'll be a handy place to tack favorite recipes, take-out
menus, frequently called phone numbers and more! Just for
fun, attach button-box buttons to thumbtacks with glue.

Spicy Hot Dog & Burger Sauce

Judith Zechman
Butler, PA

*Try this tasty sauce at your next school fundraiser
or neighborhood cookout...it's sure to be a hit!*

1 lb. ground beef, browned and
   drained
8-oz. can tomato sauce
2 c. water
1-1/2 T. Worcestershire sauce
1 T. prepared horseradish
1 t. hot pepper sauce

1 T. dried, minced onion
1 T. chili powder
1 t. dried oregano
1 t. cayenne pepper
1/8 t. nutmeg
1/8 t. salt

Combine all ingredients in a large saucepan. Cover and simmer over
low heat for 30 minutes, stirring occasionally. May also be prepared in
a slow cooker; cover and cook on low setting for several hours. Serve
immediately or keep refrigerated. Makes about 5 cups.

*Corral mail, recipe clippings and family photographs in
style...cover hatboxes with pretty vintage wallpaper.*

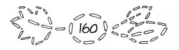

Farmhouse *Pantry*

Margaret's Chili Sauce

Brenda Conkling
Marquette Heights, IL

My mother-in-law gave me this recipe...it's wonderful when you have lots of tomatoes ripening in the garden! I like to serve some of it immediately and then freeze the rest so we can enjoy the flavor of fresh tomatoes throughout the year.

16 lbs. tomatoes, peeled and
   chopped
1 onion, chopped
1 green pepper, chopped
1/2 c. cider vinegar
1 c. brown sugar, packed

1 c. sugar
2 t. allspice
2 t. cinnamon
salt and pepper to taste
5 to 6 1-pint plastic freezer
   containers

Place tomatoes, onion and green pepper in a large Dutch oven. Add vinegar, sugars and spices; bring to a boil over medium-high heat. Reduce heat to a low simmer. Cook for 1-1/2 to 2 hours, stirring often, until cooked down and thickened. Add salt and pepper to taste. Remove from heat; cool slightly and spoon into containers. Place in freezer. Makes 5 to 6 jars.

Tin cans with colorful, vintage-style labels make clever holders for potted plants.

Savory Steak Butter

Cathy Clemons
Narrows, VA

*Dad always loved extra-juicy steaks and chops...no dry meat for him!
This saucy butter was just the thing and it also added a little zing to
the flavor of the meat. Lately I've found the new chipotle-flavored hot
pepper sauce is tasty in this too.*

1/2 c. butter, softened
2 T. steak sauce
1 T. Worcestershire sauce
1 t. smoke-flavored cooking
   sauce

1/8 t. hot pepper sauce
1 clove garlic, crushed
1/2 t. seasoned salt

In a small bowl, beat together butter and remaining ingredients until
well blended. Shape into a log; wrap in plastic wrap and refrigerate.
At serving time, slice to serve on grilled steaks or chops. If desired,
plastic-wrapped log may be wrapped in aluminum foil and frozen for
up to 6 months; no need to thaw before using. Makes about 1/2 cup.

*Nostalgic food advertisements from vintage ladies' magazines
can be found at most flea markets. Choose one or several
to frame for a whimsical wall decoration.*

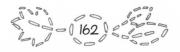

Farmhouse *Pantry*

All-Purpose Meat Marinade

*Caroline Stoltzfus
Sarasota, FL*

*This versatile marinade is delicious with beef, pork, chicken
and even fish. We especially enjoy it for marinating
cubed meats for grilled kabobs.*

1/2 c. oil	1 T. Dijon mustard
1/4 c. soy sauce	1 T. dried parsley
1/4 c. red wine vinegar	1 clove garlic, pressed
1/8 c. lemon juice	1/2 t. salt
1 T. Worcestershire sauce	1/2 t. pepper

Whisk all ingredients together. Keep refrigerated in a covered
container. To use, place 4 to 6 pieces of chicken, beef, pork or fish in
a plastic freezer bag or container and add marinade. Refrigerate or
freeze until ready to prepare. Grill meat, brushing occasionally with
marinade. Discard any excess marinade that has been used. Makes
about one cup.

*Fill uniquely shaped bottles from Grandma's pantry with herb
vinegars...you can even tuck in a fresh sprig of herbs or
herb blossoms. They'll sparkle on a windowsill.*

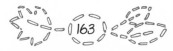

Great Chicken BBQ Sauce

Kim Faulkner
Gooseberry Patch

Why use ordinary bottled barbecue sauce? This yummy sauce can easily be stirred up with ingredients you probably already have in the pantry!

1 c. catsup
1/4 c. Worcestershire sauce
1/4 c. brown sugar, packed
2 T. cider vinegar

2 t. salt
1 t. dry mustard
1/2 t. garlic powder

Mix all ingredients together in a small saucepan. Simmer over very low heat for one hour, stirring occasionally. Use to baste chicken pieces while grilling. Makes about 1-1/2 cups.

Fill Mason jars with your own special savory sauce to give as a take-home gift. Tie on a recipe card and a BBQ brush with a bit of jute...cookout guests will love it!

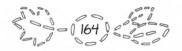

Farmhouse *Pantry*

Banana Pepper Mustard

Sharon Demers
Dolores, CO

This year our garden was bursting with banana peppers! A good friend shared this recipe with me...from now on, I will be sure to plant banana peppers every year. This mustard has a sweet-hot taste that's especially delicious with soft pretzels.

32-oz. jar mustard
32-oz. bottle cider vinegar, divided
6 c. sugar
40 to 50 banana peppers, seeded and finely chopped

9 T. cornstarch
8 to 10 1-pint canning jars and lids, sterilized

Combine mustard, 3 cups vinegar, sugar and peppers in a Dutch oven. Bring to a boil over medium heat, stirring constantly. Mix cornstarch with remaining vinegar; slowly stir into mustard mixture. Cook and stir until thickened. Remove from heat and pour into hot sterilized jars, leaving 1/2-inch headspace. Wipe rims; secure with lids and rings. Process for 10 minutes in a boiling water bath. Set jars on a towel to cool; check for seals. Makes 8 to 10 jars.

A cabin with plenty of food is better than a hungry castle.
-Irish Saying

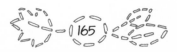

Rosemary Crumb Coating

Margaret Welder
Madrid, IA

This recipe came from my sister-in-law. It is a scrumptious way to cook chicken or pork chops...and much healthier than frying!

1-1/2 c. dry bread crumbs
1/2 c. all-purpose flour
2 T. salt
1 T. dried rosemary

1 T. paprika
1/4 t. onion powder
3 T. oil

Combine all ingredients; toss to mix. May be kept refrigerated indefinitely in a covered container. To use, moisten chicken pieces or pork chops with water; roll in crumbs. Place on a baking sheet lined with aluminum foil that has been sprayed with non-stick vegetable spray. Bake at 350 degrees for 25 to 35 minutes, until done. Discard any excess crumbs that were used to coat the meat. Makes about 2 cups.

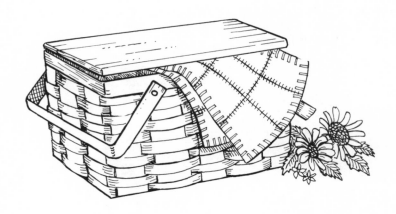

Thrift shops always have heaps of gently used baskets. Keep several on hand and you'll be ready to put together a gift at a moment's notice. Tuck in a loaf of fresh-baked bread or a dozen cookies wrapped up in a tea towel...oh-so thoughtful!

Farmhouse *Pantry*

Stacie's Spaghetti Sauce

*Stacie Allison
Fredericksburg, VA*

This is the recipe my mother used back in the days before you could buy spaghetti sauce in a jar at any grocery. It is still my favorite and so easy to make. Serve over your favorite pasta.

1 onion, chopped
1 green pepper, chopped
1 T. olive oil
1 lb. ground beef
28-oz. can chopped tomatoes

15-oz. can tomato sauce
6-oz. can tomato paste
1 T. Worcestershire sauce
1 t. garlic powder
salt and pepper to taste

In a large skillet or stockpot over medium heat, sauté onion and green pepper in oil until tender. Add ground beef and cook until browned; drain. Stir in remaining ingredients. Reduce heat to low; cover and simmer for at least one hour, stirring occasionally. Makes 4 to 6 servings.

A tall old-fashioned milk can is perfect for holding umbrellas inside the back door.

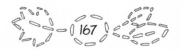

Grandma Ginny's Hot Dog Sauce

Wendy Chapman
Barboursville, WV

*This yummy recipe was handed down to me from my grandma.
It's a "must" at any family picnic! This sauce freezes well in
small containers to be reheated later in the microwave.*

2-1/2 lbs. lean ground beef	24-oz. bottle catsup
1 onion, chopped	2-1/2 T. chili powder
2 c. water	1 t. ground cumin

Combine ground beef, onion and water in a large saucepan. Bring
hamburger to a boil over medium heat and stir to crumble meat.
When meat is browned, add remaining ingredients; stir together.
Simmer on low heat for 2-1/2 hours, stirring occasionally. Makes 8 to
10 cups.

*Share your favorite tried & true recipes with a new bride
who's just learning to cook. Jot down recipes on individual
cards, along with your special touches or hints for success. Slip
the cards into the pages of a mini photo album and tie with a
homespun ribbon. She'll think of you whenever she uses it!*

Farmhouse *Pantry*

Dad's Sweet Mustard

Kathy Majeske
Denver, PA

This recipe has been in my dad's family for several generations. Dad loves to make it at Christmastime to go along with homemade pork sausage from a small hometown meat market. This mustard has a little zing to it...just the way we like it!

1 c. dry mustard
1 c. sugar

3 T. all-purpose flour
1 c. cider vinegar

Mix together mustard, sugar and flour in a bowl; set aside. Heat vinegar until hot, without boiling; add to dry ingredients. Pour into a blender; process until mixed. Store in a covered jar in the refrigerator. Makes about 3 cups.

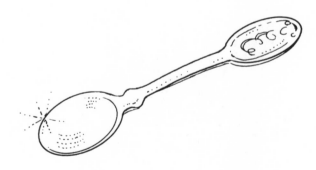

Silver-plated baby spoons are ideal for serving up dollops of mayonnaise, preserves, chutney and other condiments. Polish up Bobby and Janie's almost-forgotten little spoons or scoop up vintage finds at a tag sale.

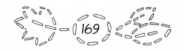

Charlotte's Hot Endive Dressing *Melody Chencharick*
Julian, PA

This was a special favorite of my father's...baked ham served with Mom's hot endive dressing. It is delicious spooned over mashed potatoes! She always prepared this in her trusty old cast-iron skillet.

1/3 c. cider vinegar
3/4 c. water
1 lb. bacon
2 eggs, beaten

1 c. sugar
2 T. cornstarch
2 T. mustard
1 head endive, chopped

Combine vinegar and water; set aside. In a skillet over medium heat, cook bacon until crisp. Remove bacon from skillet, reserving drippings. Crumble bacon into bits and set aside. Add eggs to drippings in skillet over low heat; cook and stir until scrambled. Add vinegar mixture to skillet; stir until well blended. Mix together sugar, cornstarch and mustard; add to skillet. Add endive and cook until softened, about 5 minutes. Serves 4 to 6.

Don't pass up a pretty sugar bowl just because it has lost its lid...turn it into a sweet flower vase. Slip a block of floral foam inside and arrange short-stemmed marigolds or zinnias in the foam.

Farmhouse *Pantry*

Jo's Poppy Seed Dressing

Marion Sundberg
Ramona, CA

My Aunt Jo made this dressing whenever we went to her house or she came to ours. It is scrumptious on any kind of salad. For a lighter dressing, substitute one cup of plain yogurt for one cup of the mayonnaise.

2 c. mayonnaise
2/3 c. white vinegar
1 c. sugar

2 to 3 T. poppy seed
2 t. mustard

Combine all ingredients and whisk together until smooth. Keep refrigerated in a covered container. Makes 12 servings.

Half-pint glass milk bottles make fun containers for serving salad dressings. Fill each bottle with a different variety of dressing and set them around the table, or place bottles in a wire milk carrier...so clever!

Bread & Butter Pickles

Rhonda Hauenstein
Tell City, IN

When I was growing up, we canned everything we grew in our family garden. Canning pickles was such fun! I liked slicing the pickles, so that was my "job." Now my daughter, Erika, and I can pickles every summer for my parents.

4 lbs. pickling cucumbers, sliced
3 to 4 onions, sliced
2 green peppers, sliced into
   strips
1/2 c. canning salt
3 c. cider vinegar

5 c. sugar
1-1/2 t. turmeric
1-1/2 t. celery seed
2 T. mustard seed
6 1-quart canning jars and lids,
   sterilized

Combine cucumbers, onions, green peppers and salt in a large bowl or crock. Add ice water and ice to cover; let stand for 3 hours. Drain; place in a large kettle and set aside. Combine vinegar, sugar and spices; stir well and pour over cucumber mixture. Bring to a boil over medium-high heat. Reduce heat and continue cooking until cucumbers turn a deep yellow color. Remove from heat and fill hot sterilized jars, leaving 1/2-inch headspace. Wipe rims; secure with lids and rings. Process for 20 minutes in a boiling water bath. Set jars on a towel to cool; check for seals. Makes 6 jars.

Trying your hand at pickle making? Don't get into a pickle! For best results, ask for a pickling variety of cucumbers at the farmers' market rather than using regular salad cukes from the supermarket.

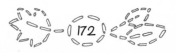

Farmhouse *Pantry*

Picnic Sweet Pickles

Ruie Richardson
Marinette, WI

This is such an easy way to have your own "homemade" pickles!
Add some red pepper flakes or tuck in some whole peeled
garlic cloves to suit your own taste.

32-oz. jar whole dill pickles,
    drained
2 c. sugar
1/4 c. white vinegar

1/4 c. water
5 whole cloves
2 to 3 1-inch cinnamon sticks

Rinse pickles well. Trim off ends of pickles, slice into chunks and return to jar; set aside. Mix remaining ingredients in a saucepan over medium heat. Simmer for 5 minutes; do not boil. Pour mixture over pickles in jar; seal jar. Let stand at room temperature for 24 hours before refrigerating. Makes one quart.

Wouldn't family members love a jar of pickles made from
Mom's tried & true recipe? Dress up the jar with a nostalgic
label. Color photocopy her handwritten recipe on cardstock
and cut out with decorative-edged scissors. Glue to the jar
and tie rick rack around the lid...so thoughtful!

Farmhouse Beet Relish

*Kelly Masten
Hudson, NY*

This relish is served every year at the local Evangelist church's Dutch Supper. It is absolutely delicious...they ALWAYS sell out well before the last seating! I was finally able to talk one of the senior members into sharing the recipe with me. It can be served as a side dish, spooned onto your favorite hoagie or used as a hot dog relish...no matter how you serve it, it is sure to be a hit!

4 c. beets, cooked, peeled and
   chopped
4 c. onions, chopped
1 T. salt
1 T. prepared horseradish

1-1/2 c. sugar
3 c. white vinegar
3 to 4 1/2-pint canning jars and
   lids, sterilized

In a large heavy saucepan, combine all ingredients. Bring to a boil over medium heat. Turn heat to medium-low and simmer for 10 minutes, stirring until sugar dissolves. Remove from heat. Ladle relish, while boiling hot, into hot sterilized jars, leaving 1/8" headspace. Wipe rims; secure with lids and rings. Allow to cool completely. Store in refrigerator until ready to use, up to 4 weeks. If desired, for longer shelf-life, process jars for 15 to 20 minutes in a boiling water bath immediately after applying lids. Set jars on a towel to cool; check for seals. Makes 3 to 4 jars.

Show off ruby-red beet relish in Mom's antique cut-glass compote. When washing cut glass, add a little white vinegar to the rinse water...the glass will really shine!

Farmhouse *Pantry*

Refrigerator Pickles

Kay Barg
Sandy, UT

Super simple...a great recipe for first-time pickle makers.

3 c. cucumbers, peeled and
　sliced
1 onion, thinly sliced
3/4 c. sugar

2/3 c. white vinegar
1/2 t. celery seed
1/2 t. mustard seed
1/4 t. salt

Mix cucumbers and onion in a glass or plastic bowl; set aside. Stir remaining ingredients together in a microwave-safe container. Microwave on high for 3 minutes, stirring after 2 minutes. Pour over cucumber mixture. Cover and refrigerate for 24 hours before serving, to blend flavors. Keep refrigerated. Makes one quart.

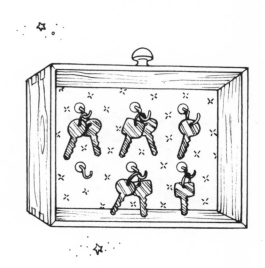

A small drawer from an old end table or dresser makes a useful key keeper to hang near the back door. Paint the drawer as you like or découpage with clippings. Add cup hooks inside to hold keys and a hanging wire on the back...an easy organizer!

Gooseberry Conserve

Angie Stone
Argillite, KY

Serve with roast chicken or turkey...yummy!

3 lbs. gooseberries, stems
  removed
3 lbs. sugar
16-oz. pkg. raisins

juice and zest of 3 oranges
2 c. nuts, chopped or broken
4 1-pint canning jars and lids,
  sterilized

Combine all ingredients except nuts in a large heavy saucepan. Bring
to a boil over medium heat, stirring until sugar dissolves. Reduce heat
and cook until thick, stirring frequently. Mix in nuts. Spoon into hot
sterilized jars, leaving 1/4-inch headspace. Wipe rims; secure with lids
and rings. Process in a boiling water bath for 10 minutes; set jars on a
towel to cool. Check for seals. Makes 4 jars.

*A butter dish makes a delightful mini windowsill garden. Turn
over the lid, set it on the butter dish, fill with soil and plant
with a tiny, low-growing herb like thyme or chamomile.*

Farmhouse *Pantry*

Candy Apple Jelly

Linda Vogt
Las Vegas, NV

*My friends & family love this sparkling red jelly so much that they
return the empty jars to remind me to make some more for them!*

4 c. apple juice or cider
1/2 c. red cinnamon candies
1-3/4 oz. pkg. fruit pectin

4-1/2 c. sugar
3 1-pint canning lids and jars,
  sterilized

Combine apple juice or cider, candies and pectin in a large heavy
saucepan. Bring to a full boil over high heat, stirring constantly. Stir in
sugar and return to a full boil. Boil for 2 minutes, stirring constantly.
Remove from heat. Skim off foam and and any unmelted candies.
Pour hot liquid into hot sterilized jars, leaving 1/4-inch headspace.
Wipe rims; secure with lids and rings. Process in a boiling water bath
for 5 minutes; set jars on a towel to cool. Check for seals. Makes
3 jars.

Add a spatterware finish to a decorative thrift-store wooden
bowl. Paint the outside of the bowl with acrylic craft paint and
let dry. Dip the bristles of a dry toothbrush into a contrasting
color of paint. Blot on a paper towel to remove excess paint,
then pull your thumb across the bristles to spatter
the paint...quick & easy speckles!

Cranberry-Tomato Chutney

Debi DeVore
Dover, OH

The tangy flavor of this quick-to-make chutney perfectly complements roast pork. For a delightful appetizer to serve with crackers, spoon some chutney over a block of cream cheese.

5 c. cranberries
28-oz. can crushed tomatoes
1 c. golden raisins

3/4 c. sugar
1 t. salt
3/4 t. ground ginger

Combine all ingredients in a large heavy saucepan over medium heat. Bring to a boil. Reduce heat; cover and simmer for 20 to 25 minutes, stirring occasionally, until cranberries and raisins are tender. Transfer to a covered container; cool. Refrigerate for 2 to 3 days before serving. Keep refrigerated. Makes 6 cups.

Old-fashioned canning jars in all sizes are easy to find at tag sales and flea markets...use them for vases, tumblers and kitchen storage.

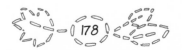

Farmhouse *Pantry*

Jezebel Raisin Sauce

Ellen Folkman
Crystal Beach, FL

*This sauce is absolutely delicious with baked ham. I found this recipe
before I was married and have been using it for nearly 20 years.
It's very easy to make...I hope you'll give it a try!*

1 c. sugar
1/2 c. water
8-oz. jar currant jelly
1 c. raisins, chopped
2 T. vinegar
1 T. Worcestershire sauce

1/2 t. salt
1/8 t. pepper
1/4 t. cinnamon
1/8 t. ground cloves
1/8 t. ground ginger

Combine sugar and water in a large saucepan over medium heat.
Bring to a boil; boil for 2 minutes, stirring until sugar dissolves. Add
remaining ingredients; reduce heat to medium and cook until blended.
Serve hot. Refrigerate any leftovers; reheat before serving. Makes
2 cups.

*A primitive painted three-legged milking stool
makes a delightful plant stand.*

Oregon Jewel Jam

Ellie Brandel
Milwaukie, OR

My husband and I bought a case of peaches from a roadside fruitstand on our honeymoon. This recipe was given to us by the farmer, and now I make it every year and think of our memorable vacation.

4 c. peaches, peeled and
    chopped
7 c. sugar
1/2 c. water
20-oz. can crushed pineapple

juice and zest of 1 lemon
4-oz. jar maraschino cherries,
    drained and finely chopped
6 1/2-pint canning jars and lids,
    sterilized

Mix peaches, sugar, water, pineapple with juice, lemon juice and zest in a large kettle. Cook over low heat for one hour, stirring frequently. Remove from heat; let stand for 5 minutes. Stir in cherries. Spoon into hot sterilized jars, leaving 1/4-inch headspace. Wipe rims; secure with lids and rings. Process in a boiling water bath for 10 minutes; set jars on a towel to cool. Check for seals. Makes 6 jars.

Homemade fruit jam isn't just for spreading on bread.
Stir a spoonful into warm breakfast oatmeal...yum!

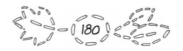

Farmhouse *Pantry*

Blueberry-Pecan Relish

Jill Ball
Highland, UT

*A jar of this sweet, nutty relish makes a beautiful gift that looks like
you spent a lot of time making it...that's your little secret!*

16-oz. pkg. frozen blueberries,
  thawed and drained
1 apple, cored, peeled and
  coarsely chopped
1 c. pecans, finely chopped
1/2 c. sugar

2 t. cider vinegar
1 t. allspice
1/2 t. cinnamon
4 t. lemon juice
3 to 4 1-pint canning jars and
  lids, sterilized

In a large heavy saucepan, combine all ingredients except lemon juice.
Bring to a boil over medium heat, stirring constantly. Remove from
heat; stir in lemon juice. Spoon into hot sterilized jars, leaving
1/8" headspace. Wipe rims; secure with lids and rings. Process jars for
5 minutes in a boiling water bath. Set jars on a towel to cool; check
for seals. Relish may also be kept refrigerated, without processing,
for 2 to 3 weeks. Makes 3 to 4 jars.

*Whip up a chalkboard to hang in the pantry for jotting down
shopping lists...no more last-minute runs to the supermarket!
Simply paint a baking sheet or shallow pan with
chalkboard paint and tie on a piece of chalk.*

Fresh Herb Pesto Sauce

Colleen Hinker
Santa Rosa, NM

*Classic Italian pesto is made with fresh basil and pine nuts,
but try other tasty combinations too, like rosemary and
pecans or oregano and almonds...delicious!*

2 c. fresh herb leaves, coarsely
   chopped
6 cloves garlic, chopped
1 c. chopped nuts

1/2 c. plus 1 T. olive oil, divided
1/2 t. salt
3/4 c. grated Parmesan or
   Romano cheese

Mix herbs, garlic, nuts, 1/2 cup oil and salt in a blender. Process until
smooth, adding a little more oil if needed to make blending easier.
Transfer to a bowl and stir in grated cheese. Refrigerate in an airtight
container or spoon into ice cube trays and freeze for later use. Makes
about 1-1/2 cups.

*Some yummy ways to enjoy pesto sauce...serve with meat
or fish. Stir into hot pasta dishes or vegetables. Add to
sour cream or mayonnaise to make a dressing.*

Farmhouse *Pantry*

Homemade Tartar Sauce

Barb Stout
Gooseberry Patch

You can whip up this fresh tartar sauce in a jiffy.

1 c. mayonnaise
2 T. dill pickles, chopped
2 T. green olives with pimentos,
    chopped
1 T. onion, grated

1 T. fresh parsley, chopped
1 T. capers
1 T. lime or lemon juice
1/4 t. garlic salt

Combine all ingredients; mix well. Cover and refrigerate until serving time. Makes about 1-1/2 cups.

Stir up some fish-fry mix the next time Dad heads for a
fishing trip. Combine 2 cups yellow cornmeal, 2 tablespoons
lemon-pepper seasoning, a tablespoon of garlic salt and a
teaspoon of pepper; store in a covered container. To use, coat
fish fillets and let stand for several minutes, then deep-fry
until golden, 7 to 10 minutes. Serve with lemon
wedges and tartar sauce...delectable!

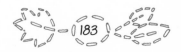

Cranberry-Jalapeño Relish

Gloria Robertson
Midland, TX

We enjoy this relish served as an appetizer...
its zingy flavor really wakes up a turkey dinner too!

1 c. water
1 c. sugar
1/4 t. salt
12-oz. pkg. cranberries
3 jalapeño peppers, seeded and
    chopped

1/4 c. fresh cilantro, chopped
1 apple, cored and grated
8-oz. pkg cream cheese
crackers, tortilla chips

Bring water, sugar and salt to a boil in a large saucepan over medium heat. Add cranberries. Reduce heat; simmer until cranberries pop and sauce thickens, stirring occasionally. Add jalapeños, cilantro and apple; stir gently to mix. Chill and serve spooned over a block of cream cheese. Serve with crackers or tortilla chips. Relish may be stored in freezer containers until needed. Makes 4 cups.

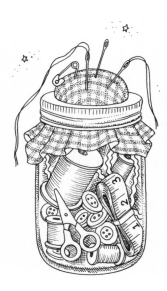

Create a sweet mini sewing kit..it's so handy! You'll need a pint-size Mason jar with a two-part lid. Pad the flat lid piece with cotton batting, cover with a circle of fabric and slide on the jar ring. Fill the jar with needles & thread, tiny scissors and a few spare buttons, screw on the lid and it's ready to use!

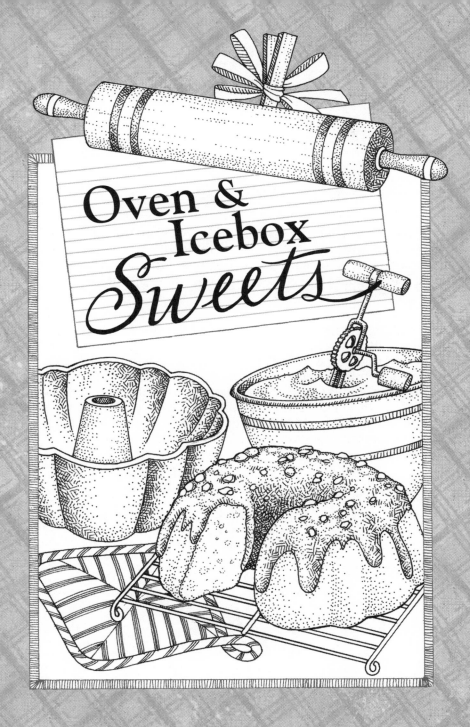

Oven &
Icebox
Sweets

Chocolate Icebox Cake

Joan Trefethen
Fairborn, OH

Surprise...it's pudding! This easy dessert is a family favorite.

3.4-oz. pkg. cook & serve
  vanilla pudding
3.4-oz. pkg. cook & serve
  chocolate pudding
3 c. milk, divided

2 sleeves graham crackers,
  divided
Garnish: whipped cream,
  chocolate sprinkles

Prepare pudding mixes separately as packages direct, using
1-1/2 cups milk for each one. Let puddings cool slightly. Line the
bottom of an ungreased 13"x9" baking pan with whole crackers.
Line sides of pan with halved crackers. Spoon vanilla pudding over
crackers. Cover with another layer of whole crackers; spoon chocolate
pudding over crackers. Crumble remaining crackers over top.
Refrigerate until chilled. At serving time, dollop individual portions
with whipped cream; garnish with sprinkles. Serves 8 to 10.

Create charming cupcake stands from tag-sale teacups and
saucers. Invert each teacup and glue its saucer on top
with epoxy glue. So clever!

Oven & Icebox *Sweets*

Amish Cream Pie

Kristen Cook
Avon Lake, OH

My younger sister and I love to visit Ohio Amish country. We always eat at one of the Amish-owned restaurants. On one trip, we tried this old-fashioned cream pie. It was so delicious, we started making trips just for the pie! We started experimenting in our own kitchens and we finally put together this recipe. We're happy to share it with everyone.

1/3 c. all-purpose flour
1/2 c. butter, melted
1 c. brown sugar, packed
1 pt. whipping cream

9-inch pie crust or graham
    cracker crust
Garnish: whipped cream

In a large bowl, blend flour into melted butter. Add brown sugar; mix thoroughly. Add cream and stir until well blended. Pour into crust. Bake at 375 degrees for 50 to 55 minutes, until center is jiggly but not liquid. Cool. Serve with whipped cream. Serves 6 to 8.

Nothing says farm-fresh flavor like dollops of whipped cream on a homemade dessert. It's easy too. In a chilled bowl, with chilled beaters, whip one cup of whipping cream until soft peaks form. Mix in 2 teaspoons sugar and 2 teaspoons vanilla extract.

Old-Fashioned Rice Pudding

Gretchen Hickman
Galva, IL

My grandmother was an excellent country cook...this recipe is hers.

5 c. cooked rice
3 c. evaporated milk
1-1/3 c. brown sugar, packed
6 T. butter, softened

4 t. vanilla extract
1 to 2 t. nutmeg
6 eggs, beaten
1 to 2 c. raisins

Combine all ingredients; pour into a lightly greased slow cooker. Cover and cook on low setting for 4 to 6 hours, or on high setting for one to 2 hours. Stir after first 30 minutes. Serves 4 to 6.

Vanilla-Almond Coffee

Kathy Grashoff
Fort Wayne, IN

A cup of this coffee warms you right up on a chilly day!

1 lb. regular or decaf ground
   coffee

2 T. vanilla extract
2 T. almond extract

Place ground coffee in a large jar with a tight-fitting lid. Add extracts; cover and shake well. Cover and store in refrigerator. Prepare ground coffee as usual. Makes one pound.

Don't hide a pretty glass cake stand in the cupboard! Use it to show off several of Mom's best dessert plates or arrange colorful, seasonal fruit on top.

Oven & Icebox *Sweets*

Graham Cracker Apple Crisp

Evie Prevo
Livermore, CA

This dessert was a sweet tradition at our family's holiday dinners as well as at other times of the year. It's a little different because it uses graham crackers in the topping instead of oats. It is the only kind of apple crisp Mom ever made for us...Grandma made it too.

8 Granny Smith apples, cored,
   peeled and sliced
1/2 c. water
1-1/4 c. sugar, divided
1 c. graham cracker crumbs

1/2 c. all-purpose flour
1 t. cinnamon
1/8 t. salt
1/2 c. butter, melted

Arrange apple slices in a buttered 11"x7" baking pan. Use more or less apples depending on their size; pan should be nearly full to the top but not heaping. Mix water and 1/2 cup sugar together; sprinkle over apples. Mix remaining sugar, graham cracker crumbs, flour, cinnamon and salt and sprinkle over apples. Drizzle melted butter evenly over topping. Bake at 450 degrees for 10 minutes; lower heat to 350 degrees and bake for an additional 40 minutes. Serves 8 to 10.

Core apples and pears in a jiffy...cut in half,
then use a melon baller to scoop out the core.

Apple Butter Roly-Poly

Lori Zolla
Friedens, PA

*This family recipe was originally made by my maternal grandmother,
Stella. It never lasts long at my house! It's especially
scrumptious made with homemade apple butter.*

2-1/2 c. all-purpose flour
1 t. salt
1 c. shortening
1/4 c. water

4 T. butter, softened and divided
1 c. apple butter, divided
4 t. sugar, divided

In a medium bowl, combine flour and salt. Cut in shortening and mix
with a fork until mixture is fine and crumbly. Sprinkle in water until
all flour is moistened and pastry almost cleans side of bowl, using
more or less water as needed. Divide pastry into two equal portions.
Roll out one portion between 2 sheets of wax paper into an 18-inch
by 8-inch rectangle. Peel off top sheet of wax paper. Spread dough
with 2 tablespoons butter; spread 1/2 cup apple butter over butter,
spreading within one inch of edges. Sprinkle 2 teaspoons sugar on
top of apple butter. Roll pastry up into a log, starting at one of the
short ends. Pinch ends shut; place seam-side down in an ungreased
13"x9" baking pan. Repeat to make a second log. Bake at 425 degrees
for 30 minutes, or until lightly golden. Cool; cut logs into one-inch
slices. Makes 2 logs, 10 servings each.

*Serve up fruit crisps or pies
in a yummy new way...layer
spoonfuls in tall parfait glasses,
layered with sweetened whipped
cream and crunchy toasted nuts
or even crushed granola.*

The Best Blondies

Elizabeth Cisneros
Chino Hills, CA

*For an extra-special dessert, serve squares topped with
a scoop of butter brickle ice cream...delicious!*

1 c. butter, melted
2 c. brown sugar, packed
2 eggs, beaten
2 t. vanilla extract
2 c. all-purpose flour
1/2 t. baking powder

1/4 t. salt
1 c. chopped pecans
1 c. white chocolate chips
3/4 c. toffee or caramel baking
  bits

Line a 12"x9" baking pan with parchment paper. Spray sides of pan with non-stick vegetable spray and set aside. In a large bowl, mix together butter and brown sugar. Beat in eggs and vanilla until mixture is smooth. Stir in flour, baking powder and salt; mix in pecans, chocolate chips and baking bits. Pour into prepared pan and spread evenly. Bake at 375 degrees for 30 to 40 minutes, until set in the middle. Allow to cool in pan before cutting into squares. Makes one dozen.

*If you see a vintage cake pan with its own slide-on lid at a tag
sale, snap it up! Not only is it indispensible for toting frosted
bar cookies to a party, it also makes a clever lap tray for kids
to carry along crayons and coloring books on car trips.*

French Silk Chocolate Pie

Linda Mercer
Shelbyville, TN

*My grandmother and mother used to make these light, refreshing
pies for every family gathering...such sweet memories!*

1/2 c. butter
3/4 c. sugar
2 eggs
2 1-oz. sqs. unsweetened
   baking chocolate, melted and
   cooled

8-oz. container frozen whipped
   topping, thawed
9-inch pie crust, baked and
   cooled, or chocolate graham
   cracker crust

In a large bowl, blend together butter and sugar until light and
creamy. Add eggs, one at a time; beat for 5 full minutes with an
electric mixer on medium speed. Add melted chocolate and blend; fold
in whipped topping. Spoon into crust; refrigerate for at least 4 hours.
Makes 6 servings.

For an extra-special gift, wrap up a jar of homemade jam
in a lacy vintage handkerchief and tie it with a ribbon.

Oven & Icebox *Sweets*

Walnut Fudge Cake

Wendy Lee Paffenroth
Pine Island, NY

For double fudgy deliciousness, I like to microwave some fudge frosting
in a coffee mug for about 20 seconds and pour it over the cooled cake.
Decorate the top with more crushed walnuts...yum!

3 eggs, beaten
1/4 c. oil
1/3 c. sour cream
1/2 c. coffee, brewed and cooled

18-1/2 oz. pkg. dark fudge cake
   mix
1/2 c. walnuts, ground
Optional: 1 to 3 T. milk

Mix eggs, oil, sour cream and coffee until well blended. Add dry cake
mix and walnuts. If batter is too thick, stir in a little milk until a good
batter consistency is reached. Pour into a greased Bundt® cake pan.
Bake at 325 degrees for 45 minutes, or until cake pulls away from
sides of pan and springs back to the touch. Cool cake in pan for 30 to
40 minutes before turning out onto a cake plate. Makes 10 to
12 servings.

For blue-ribbon perfect chocolate cakes with no white streaks,
use baking cocoa instead of flour to dust the greased pans.

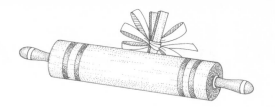

Betty's Easy Cherry Cobbler

Betty Lou Wright
Hendersonville, TN

This long-time family favorite always puts a smile on my husband's face. I usually double the recipe and bake it in a 13"x9" pan...doesn't that tell you how much he loves it? We like cherries, but feel free to substitute your favorite flavor of fruit filling.

1/2 c. margarine	1/4 t. salt
1 c. sugar	3/4 c. milk
3/4 c. all-purpose flour	21-oz. can cherry pie filling
2 t. baking powder	

Place margarine in an 8"x8" glass baking pan; set in a 325-degree oven to melt. Combine sugar, flour, baking powder, salt and milk; mix well with a wire whisk. Pour over melted margarine; do not stir. Spoon pie filling on top of batter; again, do not stir. Bake at 325 degrees for about an hour, until golden. Serve warm. Makes 6 servings.

A whistling teakettle adds cheer to any farmhouse kitchen. It's easy to remove the hard water and lime build-up in a barn-sale find. Just pour in 2 cups of white vinegar and bring to a boil. Simmer for 10 minutes, then rinse well... it'll be ready to brew up a cup of tea!

Miss Lizzie's Pound Cake

Jody Brandes
Hartfield, VA

This recipe came from a neighbor of my grandfather's back in the 1950's. I've been making it for 45 years and topping it with my mom's caramel frosting. I think you'll love it as much as I do!

1 c. butter, softened
1/2 c. shortening
3 c. sugar
1/4 t. salt
6 eggs

1 c. milk
1 t. imitation vanilla butter and
nut flavoring
3 c. all-purpose flour

Beat together butter and shortening; gradually add sugar and salt. Add eggs, one at a time, beating well after each addition; set aside. Mix together milk and flavoring; add to butter mixture alternately with flour. Spread into a greased and floured 10" tube pan. Bake at 325 degrees for one hour, until a toothpick inserted in center tests clean. Remove from pan; cool completely before frosting.
Serves 8 to 10.

Caramel Frosting:

1-1/2 c. brown sugar, packed
1/2 c. sugar
1/2 c. butter

5-oz. can evaporated milk
1 t. vanilla extract

In a saucepan over medium heat, combine all ingredients except vanilla. Cook for 15 minutes, stirring constantly. Remove from heat; stir in vanilla. Immediately spread over cooled cake.

Eggs work best in baking recipes when they're brought to room temperature first. If time is short, just slip the eggs carefully into a bowl of lukewarm water and let stand for 15 minutes...they'll warm right up.

Mom's Blackberry Crisp

Pat Gilmer
West Linn, OR

The best crisp I ever had...very simple and quick to make!
Be sure to heap the berries on because they'll cook down.

3/4 c. sugar, divided
3/4 cup plus 1 T. all-purpose
   flour, divided
1 t. cinnamon, divided
5 to 6 c. blackberries

1/8 t. salt
1/3 c. margarine
1/4 c. chopped walnuts
Optional: 1/4 t. orange or lemon
   zest

Combine 1/4 cup sugar, 4 to 5 tablespoons flour and 1/2 teaspoon
cinnamon; gently fold into berries. Spread in a greased 9" pie plate.
Combine remaining sugar, flour and cinnamon; add salt. Cut in
margarine a little at a time with a fork or pastry blender. Add chopped
nuts and zest, if using. Sprinkle topping over berries. Bake at
400 degrees for about 20 minutes, or until golden. Makes 4 to
6 servings.

Fresh-picked berries are a special country pleasure.
Store them in a colander in the refrigerator to let
cold air circulate around them. There's no need to
wash them until you're ready to use them.

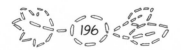

Oven & Icebox *Sweets*

Sour Cherry Pie

Sharon Demers
Dolores, CO

When I was a little girl my father would sing to me, "Can you bake a cherry pie, Sharon girl, Sharon girl?" My reply would always be a giggle and then a big "Nooo!" Well, I can finally make a cherry pie and only wish that my dad were still with us so I could serve him a big piece.

2 9-inch pie crusts
4 c. sour cherries, pitted and
    1/2 c. juice reserved
1 c. sugar
1 T. all-purpose flour

2-1/2 T. cornstarch
juice and zest of one lime
2 T. butter, diced
1 egg, beaten
2 T. whipping cream

Roll out one crust; place in a 9" pie plate. Wrap with plastic wrap and chill. Roll out remaining crust 1/8-inch thick. Cut as many one-inch-wide strips as possible to make a lattice; cut any leftover crust into leaf shapes with a cookie cutter. Place lattice strips and leaves on a parchment paper-lined baking sheet; cover with plastic wrap and chill. Combine cherries and juice in a large bowl. Sprinkle with sugar, flour, cornstarch, lime juice and zest. Toss well and pour into pie crust; dot with butter. Weave lattice strips over filling. Arrange leaves in a decorative pattern on lattice. Whisk together egg and cream; brush over lattice and edges of crust. Bake at 400 degrees for about 50 minutes, until crust is golden and juices in center of pie are bubbly. Cool slightly before cutting. Makes 6 to 8 servings.

An intricate lattice pie crust is glorious, but there's an easier way! Simply lay half the lattice strips across the pie filling in one direction, then lay the remaining strips at right angles. No weaving required!

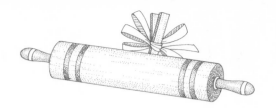

Thrifty Bread Pudding

Missie Brown
Gooseberry Patch

I started to make a bread pudding one night and realized I was out of white sugar. So...I substituted brown sugar and my husband liked it even better! Sprinkle the top with your favorite nuts.

7 hamburger buns, torn into
  bite-size cubes
1/4 c. butter, melted
3/4 c. raisins
2 t. cinnamon

5 eggs, beaten
1-1/2 c. brown sugar, packed
3 c. milk
1 t. vanilla extract
1 t. nutmeg

Combine bread cubes, melted butter, raisins and cinnamon in an ungreased 2-quart casserole dish; set aside. In a separate bowl, stir eggs and brown sugar together until sugar is dissolved. Add milk and vanilla; mix together thoroughly and pour over bread mixture. Sprinkle nutmeg over the top. Bake at 350 degrees for about 35 minutes, or until a knife inserted into center comes out clean. Serves 4 to 6.

Who doesn't remember penny candy from the corner store? Fill antique apothecary jars with a variety of candies... butterscotch drops, licorice whips, root beer barrels, caramels, jawbreakers, peppermints and lemon drops. Set out several filled jars and let everyone choose their favorite for a sweet trip down memory lane.

Sweet Fritters

Betty Gretch
Owendale, MI

A country farm recipe that has been handed down for generations. We couldn't wait for the fritters to get done...they filled the kitchen with such a sweet aroma. We ate them up as soon they were made. Enjoy them like we did, still warm from the fryer.

2 eggs, beaten
1/2 c. milk
1 c. all-purpose flour
1 t. baking powder
1 t. lard, melted

Optional: 1/2 c. apple, cored, peeled and finely diced
oil for deep frying
Garnish: powdered sugar

In a large bowl, whisk together eggs and milk. Stir in flour, baking powder and salt; mix in lard. Add diced apple, if desired. Heat several inches of oil to 375 degrees in a deep fryer. Drop batter into fryer by tablespoonfuls, a few at a time; fry until golden. Cool slightly and dust with powdered sugar; serve warm. Makes 2 dozen.

Sugar Cookie Dough

Bake up an oversized skillet cookie! Pat your favorite sugar cookie dough into the bottom of a cast-iron skillet. Bake at 350 degrees for 40 to 45 minutes, until golden on top and slightly browned on the edges. Cookie will continue to bake for a few minutes out of the oven. Turn onto a wire rack to cool slightly and cut into wedges. Yummy!

Harvard Beet Spice Cake

Betty Wachowiak
Waukegan, IL

Your friends will love trying this sweet, spicy cake...
make them guess what the "secret ingredient" is!

16-oz. jar Harvard beets
1/2 c. butter, softened
1-1/4 c. sugar
2 eggs, beaten
2-1/4 c. all-purpose flour
4 t. baking soda

1-1/2 t. allspice
1 t. cinnamon
1/4 t. ground cloves
1 c. chopped walnuts
Garnish: powdered sugar

Process beets in a blender until smooth; set aside. In a large bowl, beat butter with sugar until light and fluffy. Add eggs; beat well and set aside. Sift together flour, baking soda and spices. Add flour mixture to butter mixture alternately with puréed beets, mixing well after each addition. Fold in walnuts. Turn batter into a greased and lightly floured 9-cup Bundt® pan. Bake at 350 degrees for 55 minutes, or until cake tests done. Cool cake in pan on a wire rack for 30 minutes. Turn cake out of pan onto a cake plate. Sift powdered sugar over cake. Makes 8 to 10 servings.

A sweet addition to your baking cupboard...a heart-shaped
cake pan for cakes that say "I love you."

Oven & Icebox *Sweets*

Pineapple Upside-Down Cake

Cathy Clemons
Narrows, VA

An old favorite with a little twist. This doubly fresh-tasting cake has always been a hit at my office. Some like to say it's a good way to get your Vitamin C...really it's just an excuse to eat another slice!

6 T. butter
1 c. brown sugar, packed
20-oz. can pineapple slices,
    drained
8 to 10 maraschino cherries

18-1/2 oz. pkg. yellow cake mix
3 eggs, beaten
1/3 c. oil
20-oz. can crushed pineapple
Garnish: whipped cream

Melt butter in a 13"x9" baking pan in a 350-degree oven. Remove pan from oven; sprinkle brown sugar over butter. Arrange pineapple slices decoratively in pan; fill in spaces with cherries and set aside. In a large bowl, combine dry cake mix, eggs, oil and crushed pineapple with its juice. Beat with an electric mixer on high speed for 2 minutes. Pour batter over pineapple slices. Bake at 350 degrees for 40 minutes, or until cake tests done. Remove from oven; allow to cool 10 to 15 minutes in pan. Place a serving platter onto pan and very carefully invert cake onto platter. Serve warm or at room temperature, topped with whipped cream. Makes 16 servings.

Toss a few slices of apple in the cookie jar
to keep cookies soft and fresh.

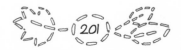

Orange Icebox Cookies

Janice Curtin
Anna, IL

My mother, Eunice, was an excellent cookie baker. This recipe is from way back in the 1950's. She always made a tin of cookies for my kids once a week when they were growing up.

1 c. shortening
1/2 c. sugar
1/2 c. brown sugar, packed
1 egg, beaten
2-3/4 c. all-purpose flour

1/2 t. baking soda
1/2 t. salt
2 T. orange juice
1 T. orange zest
1/2 c. chopped nuts

Mix together shortening, sugars and egg in a large bowl; set aside. Sift together flour, baking soda and salt; gradually add to sugar mixture. Stir in orange juice, zest and nuts. Divide dough in half; roll each half into a 2-inch-thick log and refrigerate overnight. Slice 1/4-inch thick. Place on ungreased baking sheets. Bake for 9 to 11 minutes. Makes 5 to 6 dozen.

Big potato chip tins make roomy containers for storing cookie cutters. You may even find one from a long-gone but fondly remembered hometown chip maker.

Oven & Icebox *Sweets*

Country Raisin Gingersnaps

Michelle Greeley
Hayes, VA

*My great-grandmother, Stella Carver, made these cookies in the
1930's. She was the cook at a logging camp in Michigan.*

3/4 c. shortening
1 c. sugar
1 egg, beaten
1/2 c. molasses
3-1/2 c. all-purpose flour
2 t. baking soda

1 t. salt
1 t. ground ginger
1/4 t. ground cloves
1/2 t. cinnamon
1-1/2 c. raisins, chopped
Garnish: sugar

In a large bowl, beat shortening with an electric mixer on high speed
until creamy. Gradually beat in sugar until fluffy. Add egg; beat until
blended. Reduce mixer to medium speed; beat in molasses and set
aside. Sift flour, baking soda, salt and spices; gradually add to
shortening mixture. Fold in raisins. Turn dough out onto a sheet of
aluminum foil. Wrap and refrigerate for one to 2 hours. Form into
one-inch balls and roll in sugar; place on greased baking sheets.
Bake at 375 degrees for 10 to 12 minutes, until tops of cookies are
crackled. Let stand for 2 minutes before removing cookies from
baking sheets. Makes about 3-1/2 dozen.

*Treat everyone to fresh-baked
cookies & icy cold milk...
served up in pint-size
vintage milk bottles!*

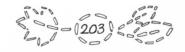

203

Wash-Day Peach Pie

Jennifer Bryant
Bowling Green, KY

*Nanny tells me that this pie got its name because it was so simple
farmwives could make it on the days they did the laundry...the
old-fashioned way! It's more like a cobbler than a pie...yummy made
with pears instead of peaches too.*

1 c. self-rising flour
1 c. sugar
1 c. milk
15-oz. can sliced peaches,
    drained

1/4 c. butter, sliced
Garnish: vanilla ice cream or
    whipped topping

Stir together flour and sugar; add milk and stir until smooth. Pour
batter into a greased 1-1/2 quart casserole dish; spoon peaches over
top. Place butter in center. Bake at 350 degrees for one hour, or until
golden. Serve warm, topped with ice cream or whipped topping.
Makes 8 servings.

Hang up an old-fashioned mini washboard where family
messages, calendars and to-do lists can easily be found.
Fabric yo-yo's hot-glued to button magnets will hold
everything in place and add a dash of whimsy.

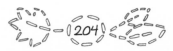

Oven & Icebox *Sweets*

Telephone Cookies

Julie Gavin
San Antonio, TX

We've been making these scrumptious no-bakes for nearly 50 years now. They came about through my grandma's telephone eavesdropping. She shared a party line with her neighbors as they lived out in the country. One day when Grandma wanted to use the phone, she picked up the receiver and heard the neighbor lady giving out a recipe. She quickly wrote down the ingredients and directions, but never caught the name of the recipe. We love these cookies...kids love to make them too!

2 c. powdered sugar, divided
2 T. butter, softened
1 c. creamy peanut butter

1-1/2 c. crispy rice cereal
3 T. milk
1 c. sweetened flaked coconut

Combine one cup powdered sugar, butter, peanut butter and cereal in a large bowl. Mix with your hands and form into walnut-size balls. Place in a plastic freezer container; freeze. To make frosting, combine remaining powdered sugar and milk until smooth. Dip frozen cookies into frosting and roll in coconut. Keep stored in the freezer in a sealed container. Makes 6 dozen.

Grandma's Special Cookies

A one-gallon glass apothecary jar makes a great cookie jar. Personalize it by using a glass paint pen to add a message like "Grandma's Special Cookies" and hearts or swirls just for fun.

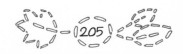

Grandma & Katie's Frozen Dessert
Jennifer Brown
Garden Grove, CA

*This used to be my birthday cake every year...I loved it! To this day
every time we make this dessert, I think of all those
birthday parties in the backyard.*

1/2 c. creamy peanut butter
1/2 c. light corn syrup
2 c. crispy rice cereal
2 c. chocolate-flavored crispy
  rice cereal

1/2 gal. vanilla ice cream,
  softened
1/2 to 1 c. Spanish peanuts
Garnish: chocolate syrup

Blend together peanut butter and corn syrup in a large bowl. Add
cereals; stir until coated. Press into the bottom of a ungreased
13"x9" baking pan. Spread ice cream over cereal mixture; sprinkle
with peanuts. Swirl chocolate syrup over top. Cover with aluminum
foil; freeze at least 4 hours before serving. Cut into squares to serve.
Makes 15 to 18 servings.

*A retro tin breadbox makes a convenient
cubby for favorite cookbooks.*

Oven & Icebox *Sweets*

Sweet Vanilla Pudding

Elizabeth Cisneros
Chino Hills, CA

There's nothing more comforting than a bowl
of warm homemade pudding!

1/4 c. sugar	2 egg yolks, beaten
2 T. cornstarch	1 T. butter
1/8 t. salt	2 t. vanilla extract
2 c. milk	1/4 t. nutmeg

In a small saucepan, combine sugar, cornstarch and salt. Stir in milk; cook and stir over medium heat until thickened. Reduce heat to low; continue cooking and stirring for 2 minutes. Place egg yolks in a small bowl. Add a small amount of hot milk mixture to yolks; stir and return all of yolk mixture to pan, stirring constantly. Bring to a gentle boil; cook and stir one minute longer. Remove from heat; add butter, vanilla and nutmeg. Let cool in pan for 15 minutes, stirring every 5 minutes. Transfer to dessert bowls; cover and refrigerate. May be served slightly warm or cold. Serves 4.

A double boiler is a "must" for melting chocolate without scorching. To be sure the water in the bottom pan doesn't boil down too low, drop in a glass marble when you fill the pan. The marble will rattle when it's time to add more water.

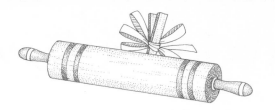

Martha's Shredded Apple Pie

Patti Walker
Mocksville, NC

Every year at Christmastime, my Grandmother Martha would make the best apple pies. The first time my boyfriend tasted her pie, he said he would definitely marry me if I could cook as well as she did. I guess I passed the test, because we have been married over 15 years! This is a family heirloom recipe that my Granny (great-grandmother) first made...don't tell my grandmother I shared it!

8 Granny Smith apples, cored,
   peeled and shredded
1/4 t. lemon juice
1-1/2 t. apple pie spice
2 9-inch pie crusts

1/2 c. butter, melted
2 c. sugar
3 eggs, beaten
nutmeg to taste

Place apples in a large bowl; toss with lemon juice and spice. Pierce unbaked crusts lightly with a fork; fill with apples. Mix melted butter, sugar and eggs; pour mixture evenly over apples. Dust the top of each pie with a dash of nutmeg. Bake at 350 degrees for 45 minutes to an hour. Allow to cool (if you can wait!) before slicing. Makes 2 pies, 8 servings each.

An apple pie without some cheese
Is like a kiss without a squeeze.
-Old saying

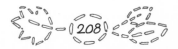

Oven & Icebox *Sweets*

Grandma's Custard Pie

Teena Hippensteel
Fort Wayne, IN

This is a recipe that my grandma made on the farm and handed down to my mom and me. We love this pie...Grandma still does too! If you wish, you can use two, 8-inch pie crusts to make two shallower pies.

4 eggs, beaten
1/2 c. sugar
1/4 t. salt
1 t. vanilla extract

2-1/2 c. milk
nutmeg to taste
9-inch deep-dish pie crust

Whisk eggs, sugar, salt and vanilla together; beat well and set aside. In a medium saucepan over medium-low heat, heat milk just until bubbles form around the edge. Stir in egg mixture; pour into crust. Sprinkle nutmeg on top. Bake at 475 degrees for 5 minutes. Reduce heat to 425 degrees and continue to bake for 15 to 20 minutes, until top is golden. Let cool before slicing. Serves 6 to 8.

If you love to bake, keep a small vintage coffee grinder on hand for grinding whole spices. The extra-fresh flavor of freshly ground cinnamon, cloves and nutmeg can't be beat.

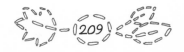

Coconut Fridge Cake

Jennifer Holcomb
Port Angeles, WA

Whenever I make this cake, I smile! This yummy recipe was given to me by one of my most favorite people in the whole world...my sister-in-law, Barb. Not only is it the yummiest cake ever, it makes me think of Barb and how lucky we are to have her in our family.

18-1/2 oz. pkg. white cake mix
16-oz. container frozen whipped
   topping, thawed

8-oz. container sour cream
1 c. sweetened flaked coconut
1 c. sugar

Prepare cake mix according to package directions, baking in two, 9" round baking pans. Cool; slice each layer horizontally in half to make 4 layers. To make frosting, mix remaining ingredients together well. Frost and stack layers on a cake plate; frost top and sides of cake with remaining frosting. Cover and refrigerate cake for one to 3 days before serving, as flavor improves with age. Serves 8 to 10.

Invite friends & family to an old-fashioned ice cream social! Set up tubs of ice cream and lots of toppings...fluffy whipped cream, peanuts, bananas, maraschino cherries, hot fudge sauce and butterscotch topping. Give a prize for the most creative sundae!

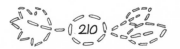

Oven & Icebox *Sweets*

Rainy Day Cookies

Mary Gentry
Pikeville, KY

A couple of these chocolate and nut-filled cookies
will cheer you up on even the gloomiest day!

1 c. butter, softened
1/4 c. sugar
3/4 c. brown sugar, packed
1 t. vanilla extract
3.4-oz. pkg. instant vanilla
    pudding mix

2 eggs, beaten
2-1/4 c. self-rising flour
12-oz. pkg. semi-sweet
    chocolate chips
8-oz. pkg. black walnuts,
    chopped

Combine butter, sugars, vanilla and dry pudding mix in a bowl; beat
until smooth and creamy. Beat in eggs; add flour gradually. A little
more butter may be added if batter seems too dry. Stir in chocolate
chips and nuts until batter is stiff. Drop by rounded teaspoonfuls,
2 inches apart, on ungreased baking sheets. Bake at 375 degrees for
8 to 10 minutes. Makes 2 dozen.

Teacups & saucers can be had for a song at tag sales. Start a
collection with a single theme...all cups with pink roses,
blue forget-me-nots or whatever strikes your fancy.
They'll be a fun topic of conversation at any tea party!

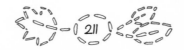

Cherry Pie Supreme

Debbie Manning
Wayland, IA

My son loves cheesecake and my husband loves cherry pie.
So I combined the two to create this delectable dessert.

21-oz. can cherry pie filling,
  divided
9-inch pie crust
4 3-oz. pkgs. cream cheese,
  softened

1/2 c. sugar
2 eggs, beaten
1/2 t. vanilla extract
Garnish: 1 c. frozen whipped
  topping, thawed

Spread half of pie filling in bottom of crust; set aside remaining filling. Bake filled crust at 425 degrees for 15 minutes, or just until golden. Remove from oven; reduce temperature to 350 degrees. In a large bowl with an electric mixer on high speed, beat cream cheese, sugar, eggs and vanilla until smooth. Pour over hot pie filling in crust; bake at 350 degrees for 25 minutes. Filling will be slightly soft in center. Cool completely on a wire rack. Spread with remaining filling; top with whipped topping. Serves 8.

A ceramic pie bird keeps juicy fillings from bubbling over in
a double-crust pie. Set it in the center of the unbaked bottom
crust and pour the filling around it. Cut a slit in the center of the
top crust and fit it carefully over the pie bird. Bake as usual and
let cool. You can lift out the pie bird when the first slice is cut.

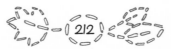

Oven & Icebox *Sweets*

Dutch Apple Pie

Christina Hubbell
Jackson, MI

A family picnic favorite that's simple to make.

2/3 c. plus 2 T. all-purpose flour, divided
1/2 c. brown sugar, packed
1/3 c. butter
6 c. tart cooking apples, cored, peeled and thinly sliced

1 T. lemon juice
3/4 c. sugar
1 t. cinnamon
9-inch pie crust

For crumb topping, combine 2/3 cup flour and brown sugar in a medium bowl. Cut in butter with a pastry blender or 2 knives until mixture is the consistency of coarse cornmeal; chill. Place apple slices in a large bowl; sprinkle with lemon juice and set aside. Combine remaining flour, sugar and cinnamon; mix well and toss lightly with apples. Turn apple mixture into unbaked crust, spreading evenly. Cover with chilled topping. Bake at 400 degrees for 40 to 45 minutes, until apples are tender. Makes 6 to 8 servings.

Save time when baking. Tuck a measuring cup into your countertop canisters. It'll be ready to scoop out flour and sugar in a jiffy.

Million-Dollar Fudge

Dana Nemecek
Skiatook, OK

This fudge recipe is my Mamaw's recipe. She passed away 20 years ago and my children never knew her, so making a pan of her fudge together is a sweet way for me to share her with them.

13-oz. pkg. milk chocolate
  candy bars, broken up
12-oz. pkg. semi-sweet
  chocolate chips
2 c. chopped pecans, toasted
  if desired

12-oz. can evaporated milk
4-1/2 c. sugar
13-oz. jar marshmallow creme
1/2 c. butter
1 t. vanilla extract

Combine chocolate bars, chocolate chips and nuts; set aside. Place evaporated milk and sugar in a large heavy saucepan; bring to a full boil over medium-high heat. Cook for 6 minutes, stirring constantly. Add marshmallow creme and butter; stir in chocolate mixture. Beat until creamy and chocolates are melted. Pour into a buttered 13"x9" baking pan. Cool; cut into small squares. Makes about 8 dozen pieces.

A primitive pie safe makes a useful mini pantry for canned goods and boxed mixes. Accent it with embroidered tea towels draped over the pierced-tin doors.

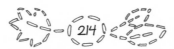

Oven & Icebox *Sweets*

Buttermilk Fudge

Sally Swift
Jacksonville, FL

During the Second World War, my family moved from Iowa to Welch Cove, North Carolina, where my father was an engineer building the Fontana Dam. We were one of many families brought from around the country to help with the war effort, so Mother had many new regional recipes to share and gather. Our next-door neighbor who was from Mississippi gave us a favorite that we still call "Ida Mattie Burns' Buttermilk Fudge." This delicious fudge became a Christmas tradition...it has been in our family now for 62 years. My children, and now grandchildren, look forward each year to this fudge.

1 t. baking soda	2 T. light corn syrup
1 c. buttermilk	1 T. butter
2 c. sugar	1 c. chopped pecans

In a large heavy saucepan, dissolve baking soda in buttermilk. Add sugar, corn syrup and butter. Cook over medium-high heat, scraping sides of pan often, until mixture reaches the soft-ball stage, or 234 to 243 degrees on a candy thermometer. Remove from heat. When pan is cool to touch on the outside, add nuts and beat well. Pour out onto a wax-paper lined paper-lined baking sheet; let stand until set. Fudge should be firm on the outside and creamy on the inside. Cut into squares. Makes 2 to 3 dozen pieces.

Cookie cutters make a whimsical valance for a kitchen window. Secure a tension rod across the top of the window and suspend cookie cutters with ribbons...so clever!

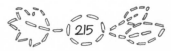

Special Hot Cocoa

Alysson Marshall
Newark, NY

*I can still remember my grandma fixing homemade hot cocoa
for me as a child...instant cocoa can't hold a candle to it!*

4 c. milk
1/4 c. baking cocoa
1/2 c. sugar
1 t. vanilla extract

1/8 t. salt
Garnish: marshmallows or
    whipped cream

Warm milk in a saucepan over medium-low heat. Add cocoa, sugar,
vanilla and salt. Stir constantly until sugar dissolves and milk is just
frothing on the top. Serve topped with marshmallows or whipped
cream. Makes 4 servings.

Marshmallow Stars

Jill Ball
Highland, UT

*My children love making these fun marshmallows for their hot cocoa...
it gives them something to do while the water is heating!*

regular-size marshmallows

Roll each marshmallow flat with a rolling pin. Cut a star shape out
with a mini cookie cutter. Drop into hot cocoa. Make as many as
you like!

*Old-fashioned salt shakers make the prettiest little containers
for dusting desserts or hot beverages with a bit of spice.*

Oven & Icebox Sweets

Family Favorite Frosting

Nichole Martelli
Santa Fe, TX

At our house, we slather this frosting on everything from cakes to cookies...it also makes a yummy filling for homemade cookie sandwiches. My husband calls it "birthday cake frosting" because he says it tastes just like the frosting on the cakes you get at the bakery.

16-oz. pkg. powdered sugar
1 c. butter-flavored shortening
2 T. water
2 t. vanilla extract

Place all ingredients in a large bowl. Beat with an electric mixer on low speed to combine. Increase speed to medium; beat for 5 full minutes. At first it won't look much like frosting, but keep the mixer going for the full 5 minutes. Makes enough to frost a 2-layer cake or a 13"x9" sheet cake.

Angel Mallow Frosting

Becky Jackson
Parkersburg, WV

My mom has made this icing for cakes since I was a little girl and I loved it! Now that I'm grown up, it's still a favorite of mine.

1/2 c. sugar
2 egg whites, beaten
2 T. water
7-oz. jar marshmallow creme
1/2 t. vanilla extract
few drops desired food coloring

Combine sugar, egg whites and water in a double boiler over boiling water. Beat with an electric mixer on high speed until soft peaks form. Add marshmallow creme; beat to stiff peaks. Remove from heat; beat in vanilla. Tint with food coloring. Makes enough to frost a 13"x9" sheet cake.

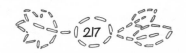

Fresh from the *Farmhouse*

Recipe: ....
Servings: ....

Copy, cut and color to share your own homemade goodies!

from the kitchen of:

Make copies of this recipe card to share your favorites with a friend!

Copy these bookmarks and use to mark your favorite recipes in this or any of your other favorite Gooseberry Patch cookbooks!

RECIPE

★ BOOK ★

PAGE

NOTES ABOUT
THIS RECIPE

★

A delicious secret the next time you make mashed potatoes... substitute equal parts chicken broth and cream for the milk in any favorite recipe.

RECIPE

★ BOOK ★

PAGE

NOTES ABOUT
THIS RECIPE

★

For tomatoes to keep their fresh-from-the-garden taste, they should always be stored at room temperature.

INDEX

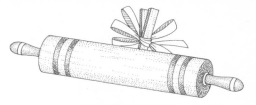

INDEX

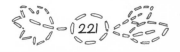

INDEX

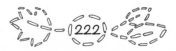

We've cooked up a whole collection of Gooseberry Patch® books!

Have a taste for more? Call us toll-free at
1-800-854-6673
We'll send you our latest catalog filled with kitchenware, handmade quilts, gourmet goodies, enamelware, mixing bowls, night lights and our very own line of cookbooks, calendars, and organizers!

Phone us:
1·800·854·6673

Fax us:
1·740·363·7225

Visit our website:
www.gooseberrypatch.com

Send us your favorite recipe!

and the memory that makes it special for you!* If we select your recipe for a brand-new **Gooseberry Patch** cookbook, your name will appear right along with it...and you'll receive a FREE copy of the book! Submit your recipe on our website at **www.gooseberrypatch.com** or mail it to:

Gooseberry Patch
Attn: Cookbook Dept.
P.O. Box 190
Delaware, OH 43015

*Please include the number of servings and all other necessary information!

farmhouse table chicken & noodles

daisies in a jar

savory pot roasts

creamery butter

calico aprons

family dinners   fresh-baked bread

U.S. to Canadian recipe equivalents

Volume Measurements

1/4 teaspoon	1 mL
1/2 teaspoon	2 mL
1 teaspoon	5 mL
1 tablespoon = 3 teaspoons	15 mL
2 tablespoons = 1 fluid ounce	30 mL
1/4 cup	60 mL
1/3 cup	75 mL
1/2 cup = 4 fluid ounces	125 mL
1 cup = 8 fluid ounces	250 mL
2 cups = 1 pint =16 fluid ounces	500 mL
4 cups = 1 quart	1 L

Weights

1 ounce	30 g
4 ounces	120 g
8 ounces	225 g
16 ounces = 1 pound	450 g

Oven Temperatures

300° F	150° C
325° F	160° C
350° F	180° C
375° F	190° C
400° F	200° C
450° F	230° C

Baking Pan Sizes

Square		Loaf	
8x8x2 inches	2 L = 20x20x5 cm	9x5x3 inches	2 L = 23x13x7 cm
9x9x2 inches	2.5 L = 23x23x5 cm	Round	
Rectangular		8x1-1/2 inches	1.2 L = 20x4 cm
13x9x2 inches	3.5 L = 33x23x5 cm	9x1-1/2 inches	1.5 L = 23x4 cm